East Lake Country Club History

Presented to Alex Smith, Secretary St Andrews Golf Club on behalf of the members of East Lake Country Club [signature] Board of Governors 8-17-90

East Lake Country Club History

Home Course of
Bobby Jones

CHARLES ELLIOTT

Foreword by FURMAN BISHER

CHEROKEE PUBLISHING COMPANY
Atlanta, Georgia
1984

Library of Congress Cataloging in Publication Data

Elliott, Charles Newton, 1906–
  East Lake Country Club history.

  Includes index.
  1. East Lake Country Club—History.
2. Jones, Bobby, 1902–1971. 3. Golfers—United
States—Biography. I. Title.
GV969.E27E45 1984   796.352′06′8758231   84-22991
ISBN 0-87797-092-0

Manufactured in the United States of America

ISBN: 0-87797-092-0

Cherokee Publishing Company
is an operating division of
The Larlin Corporation
P.O. Box 1523
Marietta, GA 30061

Dedicated to

BOBBY JONES

My favorite golfing partner and
fishing companion over many years,
and who stands immeasurably tall
in the immortal traditions of
EAST LAKE

and to

PAUL R. GRIGSBY

Who made many personal sacrifices
to save
EAST LAKE COUNTRY CLUB
from oblivion, that
those great traditions might endure.

Contents

Foreword

Bobby Jones and East Lake grew up together and became, in the eyes of golf, as one. Men of golf from about the world who have visited the United States have taken circuitous courses to find their way to Atlanta, and to see for themselves this historic club that gave us the immortal Jones. East Lake stood in their eyes as a shrine.

One of these, Percy Huggins, a magazine editor, came over from Scotland to have a look and write of it. Percy, a genuine fellow with an impressive burr, only came too soon. He should have waited a few months for Charlie Elliott's reminiscences, memoirs and historical research on East Lake Country Club to appear.

Once Bobby Jones' career as an active golfer was done, he turned to another sport and another "pro." He became a fisherman of some quality, and his teacher was Charlie Elliott, one of America's gifted writers and authorities on affairs of the Great Outdoors. Men have no better opportunity to know one another, the real person inside that skin, than when fishing. Under these circumstances Bob Jones and Charlie Elliott came to know one another, and Charlie came to absorb by direct contact some of the elegance of East Lake's past.

His history of East Lake, from Harry Atkinson to Paul Grigsby—I call him the "Cliff Roberts of Alston Drive"—reflects not only the glory of its great people. Charlie also touches those who have served the club even in the role known to sports as "unsung." From locker room attendant, to cook, to caddy master, to accountant, and no one better than he is qualified by time and association to do so.

This is a story for them, those who have served, and a tribute to those men who have held this resolute old club together and maintained East Lake's place on the great world map of golf.

Furman Bisher

Introduction

The preparation for the production of this history of East Lake Country Club began almost two decades ago. Actually, it started much further back than that. Over the many years that I played golf with Bobby Jones, and later fished with him when he was no longer able to play around a golf course, he told me many stories about his early days at East Lake and its members, and about the people who ran it.

I am indebted also to a number of other friends who had a hand in making this history possible. One was Larry Martin, President of the Atlanta Athletic Club in 1966–1967. At that time the Athletic Club was little more than two-thirds of a century old, but its achievements in athletics read like an Olympic report. In its earlier years it had developed outstanding basketball teams and swimming teams and later on, a galaxy of tennis stars and golf champions whose names were household words.

Larry Martin felt that the story of his club's growth and its worldwide achievements in athletics should be recorded for all time. Since for years I had contributed a free lance column to *Club Times*, AAC's monthly publication, Larry Martin asked me to write the history he had in mind.

With the invaluable help of Clyde S. Mingledorff, General Manager of AAC, and later M.M. (Chuck) Witherspoon, who succeeded Mingledorff when he retired, we dug back through the musty files and stacks of old records from attic to basement in both the AAC and East Lake Clubs. We talked with, and made tapes of interviews with several men who were charter members of the club, and with others who had stories of both clubs from the beginning.

In the late 1960s and early 1970s, the Atlanta Athletic Club went through a dramatic upheaval. The No. 2 golf course at East Lake was sold to a housing development group and the money put into the purchase of land along the Chattahoochee River north of Atlanta. The magnificent old downtown club was discontinued and sold and plans for the future of the Atlanta Athletic Club concentrated on shifting all properties and all activities to the newly acquired site in north Fulton County.

The No. 1, or original course, at East Lake was put up for sale. A group of Atlanta Athletic Club members, horrified at the prospect of having this world-famous property, known as the home course of such celebrated golfers as Bobby Jones, Alexa Stirling, Charlie Yates, Charles Harrison, Tommy Barnes and others, desecrated by apartment complexes, made an outright purchase of East Lake Country Club, with the intention of continuing its existence for all time as one of the world's noted country clubs. Many members of the Atlanta Athletic Club continued their membership in both clubs or resigned from AAC to join the reorganized East Lake. The story is told more fully in the pages of this book.

In the meantime, as author of the Atlanta Athletic Club history, I submitted a rough, unfinished manuscript to the new club manager and new board of directors. With it I asked for suggestions on how they thought it might be improved, what should be added to make it more complete and brought up to date.

This was in the autumn of 1973. Ten years passed and I heard nothing more from the Atlanta Athletic Club. Late in 1983 I agreed to write a history of East Lake Country Club, based on the information I had collected while researching the AAC manuscript.

This I have done, lifting those portions which apply to East Lake Country Club practically verbatim out of my earlier written text. This part of the book goes from 1904, when the idea of a country club for AAC was born, to 1968. To this has been added the progress and growth of the East Lake Country Club since that time.

East Lake Country Club
ATLANTA

I

East Lake Country Club
ITS FIRST 80 YEARS

Since East Lake Country Club was one of the early golf clubs in America, the story of this historic course should be prefaced by a few statistics and comments on the origin and introduction of the game into the states. This should give a deeper appreciation of golf and its development down to modern times, and possibly a new conception of the part East Lake has played in the growth of this fantastic sport.

No one knows exactly where the first golf course was built, or for that matter where the game started. The ancient Romans were said to have a game they called "paganica," but it smacked more of entertainment than competition. They used a small leather ball stuffed with feathers and a stick with a flattened knob on one end. There was no definite hole or goal—people simply amused them-selves when they had to make a cross-country journey afoot, by knocking the ball each time they reached it, as far and as straight ahead as possible toward their destination.

Apparently the idea spread with the Roman Empire through Europe and somewhere along the line became confined to a spec-ified area with a prescribed layout of holes. The Dutch must have had a big hand in the development, for much of the language of today's golfer stems from the Netherlands. The name of the game is thought to be from the Dutch word "kolf" which means "club." To hit his ball the Dutchman placed it on a "tuije," pronounced "toytee"; the hole itself was a "put" and the words "stuit mij," pronounded "styt-me" means "it stops me." The English changed it to "stymie."

Golf was developed in the European countries long before it

came to America. The reason was that our pioneer settlers in this country were farmers, craftsmen and tradesmen who had come here to find freedom, and who brought with them a strong adversion toward those who had depressed them, and for what they termed "frivolities" of the old country's landed nobility. Golf was a game of the idle affluent and the new Americans were so occupied with existence, they had no time for such nonsense.

With more wealthy Europeans coming to the new world, it was destined that eventually some would bring the game of golf with them. It was not until the late 1700s, however, that golf was played at all and then in only a few places in both the United States and Canada and on an indifferent basis. There is a record of a golf club at Savannah, Georgia, in 1800, but it seems to have disbanded at the start of the War of 1812 and was never reorganized.

The first permanent golf club did not make its appearance in America until 1888, ten years before the Atlanta Athletic Club was born. It was named after Scotland's famous St. Andrews course and established at Yonkers, New York. It was only a 6-hole course, with a tent for a clubhouse. The site was a 30-acre pasture, around which the pioneer golfers were allowed to knock their balls with no green fee or property rental to pay.

After four years the Yonkers clubbers decided to move their course. They did it in one day by changing the location of the tent and laying out six holes in an apple orchard. Their second move was out of the tent and into an old farm house at Grey Oaks. They arranged this into a club house and built a 9-hole course in two days.

From this humble beginning the sport of golf spread rapidly over America. The Atlanta Athletic Club was one of the first clubs in the southern states to consider adding golf to its other athletic activities. More than a dozen years after the beginning of the Yonkers Club, the Directors of the Athletic Club began to look around for the proper terrain and location which would be reasonably accessible to the members. The main club was then located on Auburn Avenue in downtown Atlanta, and was only a few years into its existence.

A site that appealed to the Directors was a low, rolling series of hills around East Lake that sprawled out in the wilds of DeKalb County, far beyond the end of the street car line, and included a part of the old Collier estate.

East Lake itself, a sparkling stretch of water surrounded by forest land, was the site of an amusement park, run by Tom Poole. It was privately owned and its chief attractions were a swimming beach, picnic tables, hot dog-popcorn-and-peanut stands, and a penny arcade where for the sum of 1¢, people could peep at such scenes as Pike's Peak, the 1889 World's Fair in far away Paris, the Eiffel Tower which opened that same year, and bathing beauties in revealing bloomers. There was also a real steamboat that huffed and puffed up and down the narrow confines of the lake to give sightseers a thrilling ride.

Early in 1904, the Georgia Railway and Power Company, parent organization of Georgia Power Company, extended the electric street car line from downtown Atlanta on to East Lake. This extension of the car line was influenced by E.P. Black and Son, and George and Forrest Adair, who had purchased a sizeable chunk of the Collier estate.

At that time most of the land was owned by Henry M. Atkinson, one of the founders of AAC, and while he never served in an official capacity, he was dedicated to the success of the club. When Atkinson died in 1939, golf writer O.B. Keeler told the story in his *Atlanta Journal* column:

"With the passing of Henry Morrell Atkinson—Harry Atkinson to so many people who loved him and cherished his friendship—the Atlanta Athletic Club lost one of its singularly distinguished charter members.

"It was back in August of 1898 that Harry Atkinson was one of 67 young men who applied for a charter for the Atlanta Athletic Club—and Harry Atkinson was a member for the rest of his long and useful life.

"It was at the dawn of the present century that the late George Adair went to Mr. Atkinson, who owned the property now occupied by the clubhouse and No. 1 course at East Lake, with the suggestion that perhaps a country club might be established, with facilities for the then new and undeveloped game of golf, if the property might be obtained within the means of the new Athletic Club.

"Mr. Atkinson's reply was brief, explicit and to the point.

"'You may have it at your own figure,' he told Mr. Adair. 'And you may put me down for a cash subscription toward the building of the clubhouse.'

"This was the first toddling step of the East Lake Country Club, on a site which Mr. Atkinson once confessed had always appealed to him as an ideal terrain and location. Atkinson had played golf in its earliest days in this country, was a bosom friend of Charles Blair MacDonald, first of the American amateur champions.

"'I could at times even visualize another St. Andrews', Mr. Atkinson said, many years after. 'But I never saw, even in the rosiest moments of the vision, an Alexa Stirling, a Bobby Jones, who were to carry East Lake to the top of the world as a home of golf, a place in the sun shared only with St. Andrews.'

"The dream was there, in Harry Atkinson's mind and heart— and the world figures of that dream evolved with all the inevitability of a natural phenomenon.

"East Lake—the Atlanta Athletic Club! As the dream materialized and the harder facts of life and the desperate era of the depression came on, Harry Atkinson, the club-member and the man of practical affairs, again stood forth as a stalwart in support, rallying the local members and friends of the Club to meet the emergency and carry on to a comfortable security commensurate with its imposing station.

"A great man, a great club member, a great sportsman, Harry Atkinson's memory is enshrined in the grateful and loving memory of the members, present and to come, of the club he loved so well, and aided so vitally in its founding and its preservation for the generations yet to come."

George Adair, AAC Vice-President under Arnold Broyles and tagged as next president, a position he was to hold for six terms, was one of the key men who arranged for the East Lake property to be turned over to AAC in July, 1904.

There is no record of when the amusement park went out of business, or whether all of its facilities were used as a part of the country club by AAC members before the new club house and golf course were complete. Apparently some of the first athletic benefits enjoyed by the members were the swimming and boating at East Lake. The first bit of construction was the addition of four tennis courts as a country club setup for what, at that time, was the most popular game among the members. Club records show that one of the first orders of business was the establishment of communication with the outside world by the addition of a telephone "duplex" line in November, 1905, at the rate of $3 per month. Then on March 6, 1906, AAC signed a contract with architect Edward E. Daugherty and builders P.J. Wesley & Sons, to construct a combination boat and bath house, as an enlargement of the facilities already located on the lake. This contract for the interim club building specified that the new addition must be completed and turned over to AAC before July 1, possibly to be ready for the July 4 celebration that year.

No dates are recorded to show when the original golf course was laid out and started. The club employed Tom Bendelow, one of the well known golf architects of that day, to do the job. The course he designed remained in play for some half a dozen years and was extraordinary, according to Bobby Jones, Jr., in that it gave a golfer the opportunity to use every wood and iron in his bag.

That first layout which started near the new club house on the knoll a few hundred feet away from the landside quarters, was vastly different from the East Lake of today. As a matter of record, the original first tee lay almost on the site of the present club house, located between the dining terrace and the lake. Play was over today's 18th green to the site of what is now the putting area north of the halfway snack bar and No. 10 tee.

The second, third and fourth holes followed about the same layout as the current 10, 11 and 12. On No. 5, the tee was about where No. 18 tee is now and play paralled the service road in the direction of the present 17th tee. From there the play was back to a green located behind the present 13th tee, and No. 7 and 8 were about the same as 13 and 14 before the last remodeling job in 1960. From the 8th green, you walked 75 or 80 yards to a tee opposite of where a swath was cut through the woods to the present 17th fairway and played a dogleg to where No. 16 green is now located. That was No. 9.

To begin the second nine, you walked across the dam to a tee located about where the current No. 6 tee stands and you played up the present No. 5 fairway to a little bench area near the fence corner just off No. 5 fairway. The 11th green was near the northeast corner of Second Avenue and Glenwood and from there you played 12 along Second Avenue to where it cornered with Alston Drive—which was really the existent No. 4 played in the opposite direction.

No. 13 was played along Alston Drive to a green in the hollow now occupied by the lake in front of today's No. 2. No. 14 was along the course of the old No. 3 before remodeling and No. 15 to a green near the big oak on the left edge of the fairway approaching the present No. 4 green.

From there you played back to today's No. 6 island hole. It was a par 5 and an island hole in those days, too, with the same canal around it. No. 17 was located on the site of the old No. 8 winter green, and from there you walked to a tee behind the current ladies' tee and played your 18th hole about as No. 9 is played today.

Bob Jones points out that the old course "was a sort of strange layout as golf courses go, because it had only two 3-par holes, the first and the third. The rest were short par 4s and 5s.

"From other standpoints it was also an interesting course. We had names for some of the holes. A couple I recall were the 16th that we knew as 'the circus ring,' because of its appearance, and the

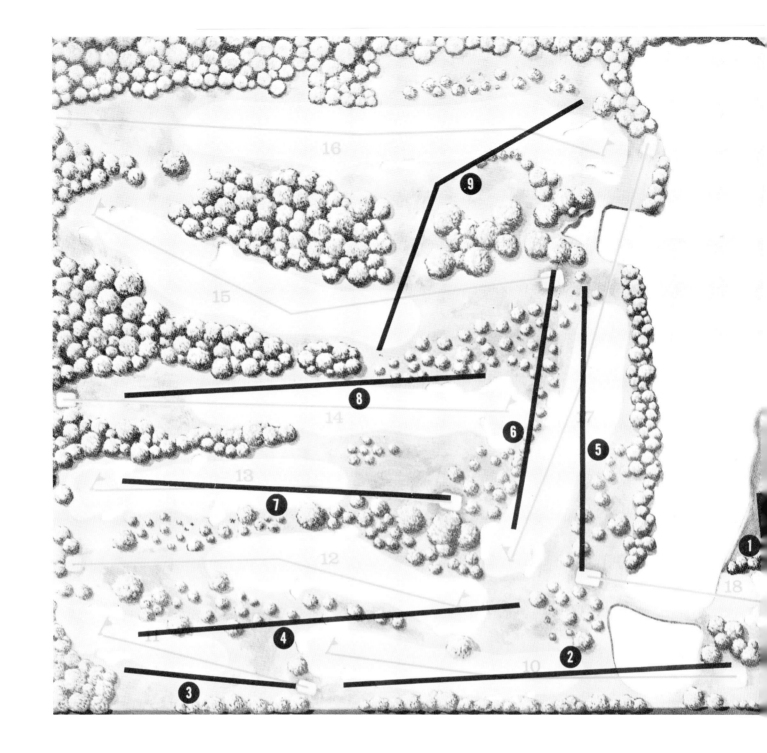

EAST LAKE'S

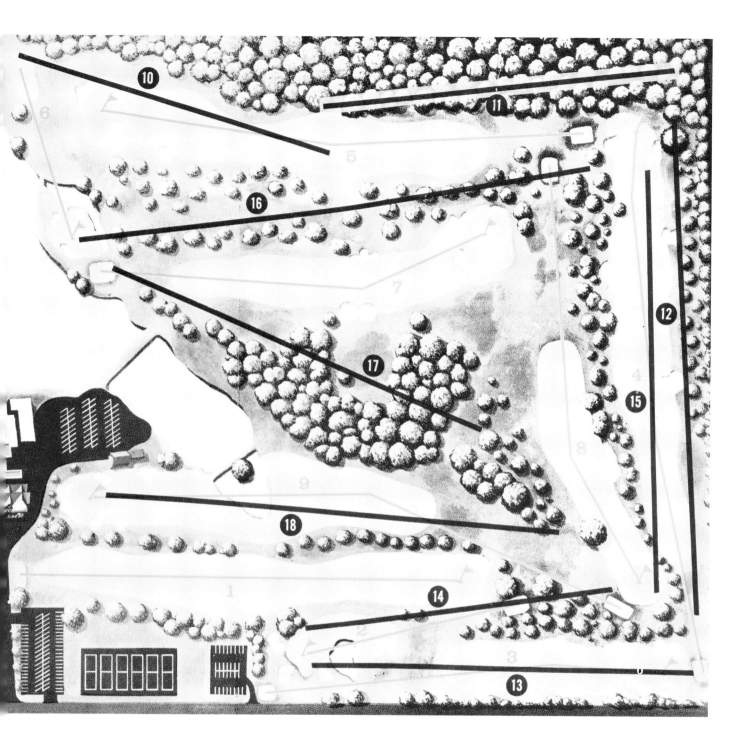

FIRST GOLF COURSE

(shown in heavy lines over present course)

14th where you had to play a shot around or over the 'spectacle bunker,' a double trap which was, of course, shaped like a pair of spectacles, or eyeglasses."

After its original construction the East Lake golf course was remodeled twice while owned by the Atlanta Athletic Club. In 1913, golf architect Donald Ross changed the holes around to approximately as they are today, and in 1959–60, George W. Cobb lengthened and expanded those holes into outstanding championship caliber for the 1963 British-American Ryder Cup Golf Matches.

The building of East Lake's initial golf layout went much slower than the two-day construction job by the Yonkers Club. More than two years were needed to hack the space for fairways, tees and greens out of the forested hillsides, to grade and shape, and grow a stand of grass on the reluctant red soil. What heavy machinery there was then, consisted of scoops, graders and mowers, all powered by mules. Most of the work to bring the new golf course into existence was done by hand, with ax and saw, and pick and shovel.

On April 13, 1907, some 15 months before the proposed opening date for the course, the club employed Harry Leslie Walker as architect to draw plans for a club house with lockers, showers and other accommodations for the golfers. Walker designed the new building to fit neatly between the starting tee and No. 18 green, on the contour of the slope above the original quarters on the lake.

When the club house and course were officially opened for use and play on July 4, 1908, only a few of the more than 500 members classified as "resident," were interested in golf. AAC remained primarily a tennis club, with only casual interest in the other athletic activities. It is interesting to note that in that year Bobby Jones was 6 years old; the National Amateur Championship was won by J.D. Travers; and the National Open Champion was Fred McLeod. (George Sargent, who was later to serve as Pro at East Lake, won the open in 1909.)

To provide food for its grand opening of East Lake and subsequently until it could install its own restaurant accommodations, AAC hired the services of a caterer.

On July 1, 1908, AAC signed a contract with the Silverman Catering Company, turning over exclusive cafe privileges, without charge, at the new country club.

This first dining arrangement at East Lake extended between July 1 and October 1 of that year.

Space assigned for serving food and beverages was the grill

room, a small dining room, and "when necessary or convenient, the porches of the club building," where "all edibles" as well as coffee, tea, chocolate and milk, were dispensed to the members.

In this contract, the club agreed to furnish the kitchen, all necessary pots and pans and other cooking apparatus, tables, linens, crockery, cutlery and silverwear—with no rental involved. The club also employed a "competent white man" who was placed in charge of the building and was instructed to receive and approve orders from the catering company, in connection with his other duties. Silverman paid one half of the club manager's salary and furnished his meals and drinks (though the contract did not specify what kind of drinks or how many). The catering company agreed to pay for all fuel and heat used in cooking and half the bill for ice delivered to the East Lake refrigerators.

The first dining facilities at the country club were open 7 days a week between six o'clock in the morning and 9:00 p.m. Hot breakfast was served from 6:00 to 9:00 a.m., hot dinners from 6:30 to 9:00 p.m., and cold lunches at all hours the cafe was open.

Members were not allowed to pay cash to the catering company for their meals or drinks, but could either sign tickets or make the payment in coupons bought at the downtown club.

Some of the small number of golfers whose names have come down to us are Frank Meador, Fulton Colville, who gave Bob Jones his first club, both Colonel and Mrs. Robert P. Jones and son Bobby, Richard Hickey, Tom Prescott, the Thomas Paines, Dr. Edgar Ballenger, Clarence Knowles, W.R. Tichenor, Alexa Stirling, George, Frank and Perry Adair, Dowdell Brown, Carlton Smith, Eston Mansfield and Fred Patterson. These ranged in age from 6 to 40, and several of the youngsters went on to make the name East Lake famous throughout the world.

"When I played golf out there," Fred Patterson related, "our foursome consisted of John Smith, Gus Gresham—We were called the Atlanta R A, which stood for 'ragged asses.' Bob Jones was a young fellow, just getting started. He could outplay us at golf, but he knew he couldn't out-talk us."

East Lake was gradually building up as a community. The new car line provided transportation from the heart of Atlanta and homes were beginning to appear in the vicinity, built by those who wanted to get away from the noise and bustle of a rapidly growing city. Many who did not live there the year round, came out during the summer to escape the heat and enjoy the lake, tennis courts and golf course.

Determined to make their new country club outstanding in every way, and to give it the most possible prestige in the growing world of golfdom, the men who had brought East Lake so far along in such a short period of time, looked around for a top professional to take charge of all activities relative to the game. From this standpoint the committee found what it considered the perfect man for the job in the person of Alex Smith.

Smith, in his middle thirties, was one of the few men who had the reputation as a "complete professional." Not only was he an outstanding shot-maker, his vast experience included course construction and maintenance, teaching and the custom manufacture of golf clubs.

Born in Carnoustie, Scotland, in 1872, he was one of five brothers who had migrated to America in the 1890s, and who played a big role in the early popularity of golf on this side of the Atlantic. His first job in this country had been as assistant pro at Washington Park in Chicago. When he came to East Lake, he already had behind him the impressive record as runner-up in the U.S. Opens of 1898 and 1901; winner of the Western Open in 1903; of the Metropolitan Open in 1905; and the winner of both the Western Open and U.S. Open in 1906. He was to go on to more championships, including a second U.S. Open in 1910. He was the first of several great pros to leave their influence and impact on the East Lake golfers and contribute to the championship quality by which AAC's first country club became known wherever the language of golf was spoken.

When Alex Smith went on to greater accomplishments in golf, the East Lake fathers went overseas, again to Carnoustie, and imported Jimmy Maiden who was a noted golfer, but more devoted to teaching the game. AAC's contract with Jimmy Maiden helps to tell the story of the times:

"WITNESSETH: That the party of the first part (AAC) has agreed to employ the party of the second part (Maiden) for the term of one year, commencing on the first day of March, 1907, at and for a monthly salary of Sixty (60.00) Dollars, payable at the end of each month.

The duties of said party of the second part under this contract of employment shall be as follows: He shall be at the country club at East Lake from 9:00 a.m. to 6:00 p.m. He shall have charge of the caddy master and caddies, and will be expected to see that said caddy master attends to his duties. He shall not charge more than $1.00 for lessons of 45 minutes each. The rates for playing shall be $1.00 for nine holes and $2.00 for eighteen holes. He shall be expected to make suggestions regarding the condition of the course to the Golf Committee. He shall have the privilege of making, repairing and selling golf clubs. (Editor's note: The contract was not quite clear whether the golf pro of that day kept the $2 green fee as part of his remuneration, or turned it in to the club.)

Finally, he shall perform such other and further duties as may be from time to time prescribed by the Golf Committee."

Perhaps Jimmy's most inestimable contribution to East Lake was the hiring of his brother, Stewart, as his assistant. Stewart made an immediate hit with the golfing set and was elected to take his brother's place as pro when Jimmy moved on.

Stewart Maiden made the first set of matched clubs that Bobby Jones ever owned. It consisted of a driver, brassie, midiron, mashie, niblick and putter. It was possibly the forerunner of the matched club set, the development of which is often credited to Jones, and came back in the days when most golfers bought clubs one at a time because of the feel, weight, swing or whatever appealed to them.

Stewart was one of the most colorful of East Lake pros over the years. He was never one of the giants of competitive golf, but a top flight teacher. His greatest claim to fame was as a model for a young fellow not yet in his teens, who followed Stewart around the course, watching his immaculate swing. The name of that youngster was Bobby Jones. The friendship between Bob and Stewart Maiden developed into affection that endured throughout all of the years of the old pro.

"Stewart," Bob Jones recalls, "was a real funny guy. He had a talent for making very pungent, irreverent, witty remarks and I remember several instances in which he commented on members in one way or another. Of one of them he said, not wholly seriously, 'Oh, he's a great player. He has only one fault; he can't hole out soon enough.'"

Once Stewart had been giving lessons to a club member for quite a while and someone asked how he was getting along with the guy. Maiden said in his rich, Scottish brogue, "I can't do a thing for him—after five minutes he's teaching me."

Another member off his game, went out to take a lesson from the pro and was asked to hit five or six balls, which he did. Then as he started to hit another, Stewart stepped up, grabbed him by the wrist and held him—he had a grip like iron—and looked him straight in the eyes and asked, "Dammit, Red, do you *have* to play golf?"

To still another member he made this suggestion, "The best thing for you to do is lay off the game for two weeks, then quit altogether."

"He was just that way," Bob Jones said. "If you did not have any particular promise, he'd give you lessons all right, but he wouldn't take much interest in you.

"Like most teaching pros, he had a knack of putting a finger on one flaw that might appear insignificant, but could make a difference in a man's game. Sometimes just one salty pointer could give a golfer a lot of help.

"At Oakmont, in the Amateur Championship, I was having trouble, shearing my tee shots off to the right and catching all the bunkers along the sides of the fairways. I was fighting for pars on every hole. Stewart heard about it and sent me a telegram, saying, 'Hit 'em hard—they'll land somewhere.'

"So I did. I kept being wild, but hitting them so hard that I knocked them over the bunkers into the adjoining fairways, which were a lot easier to play out of than the bunkers."

Stewart Maiden left East Lake, went to New York and opened an indoor golf school in the Grand Central Building, right across from Grand Central Station. In the summer he had a job instructing golf for a club in Pennsylvania's Pocono Mountains. When Peachtree Club in Atlanta was opened, he came back to the pro job there, remained there as long as he lived and was always a great favorite with the members.

"I used to follow Stewart Maiden all around the course," Bob says, "and watch him play, and unconsciously fashioned my swing after his. I never had a formal lesson from him or anyone else, either on or off the practice tee. Occasionally I'd get in trouble and ask him to watch me hit a few and make some suggestions, which was usually enough. It would take about five minutes."

By doing this, Jones developed a flawless style and vouched for its closeness to the old pro's swing by a story he told in his book, *Down the Fairway*:

"I was playing a practice round prior to the Southern Amateur Championship in Birmingham and this man, who had not seen Stewart since he left Carnoustie, was standing by Dad as I was driving off the tenth tee in the distance.

'When did Stewart Maiden get here?' he inquired.

Dad told him that Stewart was not there at all.

'You can't fool me,' was the rejoiner. 'I saw Stewart drive just now from the tenth tee. Think I don't know that old Carnoustie swing?'

After Stewart Maiden, came several pros who were popular with the growing list of golfers and who contributed their own distinctive personalities. The names of those over the intervening years before George Sargent took over the golfing duties at the country club include Frank Ball, Billy Wilson and Charles Gray.

George Sargent came to East Lake in 1932. He was one of the early touring professionals in this country and had carved a distinguished career for himself. Possibly the most noted of his victories were the U.S. Open in 1909, and the Canadian Open in 1912. He left the tour for East Lake to devote himself to teaching and to the affairs of the club, and for more than two decades remained one of the most popular pros the club ever had.

George Sargent was born in Epsom Downs, England, and started playing golf early in life. He chose this as his vocation and when he came to the United States, he was already established in his field. There was no golf circuit as such in those days, but he played in all of the major tournaments available at that time. As a matter of record, in 1909 he set the all time low score for the Open, and it held up until 1915, when Chick Evans broke it. He also established the Canadian Open record, but that score was bested the next year.

Before he took the East Lake job, George Sargent was the golf pro at many of the nation's finest clubs at that time. One was Chevy Chase in Washington, D.C., where he gave golf lessons to President Taft. From there he went to Interlachen in Minnesota, where Bob Jones won the Open in 1930. He came to East Lake from Scioto in Columbus, Ohio, where interestingly enough, Jones won the Open in 1926. Sargent remained at East Lake until his retirement in 1947, when he turned the reins over to Harold, his son and assistant at the club.

Harold was never a seriously playing pro and never followed the circuit, but he gave as much to AAC and its golfing contingent as any professional in the history of the club. His contributions to the game of golf itself have been inestimable. He was President of PGA during the years of 1958–59–60 and was as responsible as any man for bringing the 15th Biennial Ryder Cup Matches to East Lake in 1963.

Over many years Harold dedicated himself to the club, its problems and its progress. The architects of the club's future often sought his views on plans for major moves toward the improvement of AAC as well as for East Lake. One of the sparkling pieces of evidence to his administration is the fact that most of the young assistants in his golf shop went on to carve distinguished careers of their own.

Many times club members took for granted the presentable condition of their golf courses and the smooth operation which involved caddies, carts, golf bags, the locker room and even the play itself. Almost as many times they failed to recognize this was the untiring effort of the men behind the scenes, and that on this team the club pro played an impressive role.

II

The Bobby Jones Story

No history of East Lake or of the Athletic Club would ever be complete without the Bobby Jones story as it relates to those two places. East Lake was the foundation on which he built an incredible golfing record.

It is true that this story and parts of it have been told hundreds of times in the press, in magazine articles, books and recorded on film. Jones himself wrote a substantial part of it in a newspaper column that was published for many years and in a number of books. His first was *Down the Fairway* which he wrote with O.B. Keeler, *Atlanta Journal* Sports Editor, in 1927. Then he did a small book on *Rights and Wrongs of Golf* that was published by A.G. Spalding & Brothers in 1935. These were followed in 1960 by *Golf Is My Game* and in 1966 by *Bobby Jones on Golf*.

All are interesting and instructive reading, but the one that deals more fully with his early days at the game and his life and ties with East Lake was his first volume with Keeler. Much of the information here is based on this book, but also includes innumerable little incidents that Bob told the author over a third of a century, or more.

Bob's father, Col. Robert P. Jones, was on AAC's Board of Directors from 1908 to 1946, longer than any other man, and during that time he served as club president in 1937–42. Colonel Jones was a splendid athlete. His record on the baseball team at the University of Georgia was so outstanding that he was offered and signed a contract to play with the Brooklyn Club of the old National League. When his own father, and Bobby's grandfather, however, who was an influential but old-fashioned business man at Canton, heard of it, he simply vetoed the idea on the basis that he would never see his son throw his life away on such foolishness.

Bob's first memory of any sports participation was at the age of five when he played baseball with the neighborhood kids in a vacant lot across from the apartment in which his family lived on West Peachtree Street in Atlanta.

Around his fifth birthday Bob was stricken in rapid succession with most of the childhood diseases, as whooping cough and measles, prevalent at that time. To get their son out of the city and into the fresh air of the country, Col. and Mrs. Jones moved for the summer to a boarding house near the new East Lake Country Club at the end of the car line. At that time both the course and club house were still under construction, but enough of the course had been completed so that there was play on a few of the holes. That first summer the Joneses boarded with Mrs. Frank Meador in a big house that Bob described as being "about a mashie pitch from what then was the second fairway."

Frank, Mrs. Meador's son, was two years older than Bob, and the two youngsters were favorites of some of the other boarders who were much older, and who were learning the game of golf on East Lake's unfinished course. One of these older boys, Fulton Colville cut down a cleek—known today as the No. 1 iron—to Bob's size and gave it to him.

As club rules forbade youngsters the age of Bob and Frank from playing the course, the two laid out a course of their own along the roadway in front of the Meador's home. They used the road for their fairway. One hole was in the road in front of the house. The other "hole" was a deep ditch that drained into the upper end of the lake, measuring somewhat larger than the standard cup on today's greens.

"It is general opinion," Bob said, "that I never made a hole in one until 1927. As a matter of fact, I made that ditch hole many times in one, before I was six years old."

During that summer Bob's father and mother took up golf, but it was not until the following year at East Lake that the youngster's interest in the game began to really pick up.

This second summer his family again moved to East Lake for the season, but instead of living with Mrs. Meador, Col. Robert rented a building on club property. It was located between the present No. 2 green and tennis court layout. The ground story of this building was arranged to house livestock used to pull the East Lake fairway mowers and other equipment and had been used for this purpose before the house was renovated as a summer residence. It was then and forever after, as long as it stood, known as "the mule house."

It contained a dining room, living room, bedroom and bath,

and a porch around two sides, where sleeping arrangements were often set up for the warm summer nights. There was electricity but no running water and Bob remembers that one of his jobs as long as the family lived there, was hauling water by the bucketful from the residence of the Curtis family, who owned the nearest well a few houses away, up on the corner.

When they played golf this second summer, Bob's father and mother would usually allow him to follow them around the course with his clubs. By now he owned a set of three—a brassie cut down from one of his mother's clubs, a mashie discarded by his dad and his faithful cleek, with which he made most of his shots and used as a putter.

As long as he did not delay their game, Bob's parents would allow the youngster to carry his clubs and play behind them. Being afraid that they would stop him because he took too much time, Bob got in the habit of addressing his ball and hitting it with hardly a flicker of pause, thus acquiring a trait that stayed with him as long as he played golf.

This was about the time that Stewart Maiden came to East Lake, first as assistant and then as club pro. Bob was intrigued by the way the new pro swung a golf stick, and almost every time Maiden played the youngster followed him—not with his clubs, but just to watch. Then he would go home, get one of his own sticks and imitate the pro's swing. In those days the thirteenth hole was located near the Mule House and after following Maiden for a few holes, young Jones would go home to the 13th green and spend hours pitching a capful of balls to the flagstick and putting them out.

"Through all my career," he once said, "I've never been able to pitch a ball as accurately as I could pitch it to the flagstick on that green."

Jones played his first competitive golf at the age of six years, and he won the first tournament he was ever in. Mrs. Frank Meador arranged the competition between Bob, her son Frank, Perry Adair and Alexa Stirling, a neighborhood girl about Bob's age, who also developed the Maiden swing and went on to win a host of tournaments, including the Women's National Championship for three successive years.

The tournament was over six holes and Bob always believed that Alexa, and not him was entitled to the little silver cup given as a trophy. But Frank Meador had it figured that Bob won the cup—which he said was the proudest trophy of his life and the only one he ever slept with. And no doubt it helped influence the fabulous golfing career that lay ahead of him.

He won his second tournament, too—one promoted by Mrs. E.G. Ballenger. This time he met Perry Adair in the finals, and as the boys were handicapped according to their ages, Bob was given one stroke on 18 holes. The match was a 36 hole affair. He and Perry breezed around the course, with regular foursomes standing aside to let them through, in about four hours for the 36 holes, and Bob won 2 and 1 on the 35th green.

What Bob terms as his "first big cup" was the Junior Championship of AAC. At that time he was nine years old, and he walloped Howard Thorne, seven years his senior, by 5 and 4. Somebody made a picture of the little kid winner and the big 'teen age runner-up and it was published in *The American Golfer*, the first of many tens of thousands of pictures made of Bob Jones and his conquests over the years.

It was along about this period that Bob was witness to what he says was "the greatest shot" he ever saw. The impeccable Harry Vardon came with Ted Ray from England to play a match with Stewart Maiden and Willie Man, pro at the nearby Druid Hills Club.

"Ray," he wrote in *Down the Fairway*, "was right behind a tree about 40 feet in height, with thick foliage, and the tree exactly in line with the green. As Ray walked up to his ball, the more sophisticated members of the gallery were speculating as to whether he would essay to slice his shot around the obstacle to the green, 170 yards away, or "pull" it around on the other side. As for me, I didn't see anything he could do, but possibly to accept the penalty of a stroke into the fairway. He was out of luck, I was sure.

"Big Ted took one look at the ball and another at the green, with the tree between. Then without hesitation, he drew a mashie-niblick and he hit that ball harder, I believe, than I have ever seen a ball hit since, knocking it down as if he would drive it through to China. Up flew a divot the size of Ted's ample foot. Up also came the ball, buzzing like a partridge from the prodigious spin imparted by that tremendous wallop—almost straight up it got, cleared that tree by several yards and sailed up at the height of an office building, to drop on the green not far from the hole. The gallery was in paroxysms. I remember how men pounded each other on the back, and crowed and cackled and shouted and clapped their hands. As for me, I didn't really believe it. A sort of wonder persists in my memory to this day. It was the greatest shot I ever saw."

Bob Jones recalled many other conditions and incidents about the East Lake of those earlier days. Before and around the time the course was opened, there was more interest in other sports at the club than in golf. The two top athletic activities remained tennis and swimming, and at first, Jones was more dedicated to these than to golf. He especially liked tennis and competed in some of the tournaments but never collected any big laurels in that department.

He remembers that in those days Carlton Smith was Southern Tennis Champion for many years, and that at that time the champion did not have to play all the way through a tournament; that the tournament was really held to see who would have the privilege of competing with the champion in the challenge round.

The club boasted some good swimmers, too, such as Gilbert Fraser, Homer Thompson and Mariana Goldsmith, who was later Mariana Knox and prominent in women's business affairs around Atlanta. The swimming events were held in the lake over a course which he described as existing "from the old poplar tree where we used to find bream beds just opposite the dining room, up to the bridge."

One of the members about that time was H.M. Ashe who was a Canadian and apparently a man with imagination. During one real cold spell with the temperature far below freezing, Ashe had the terrace back of the club covered with water. It froze into a sheet of ice and the Canadian gave a spectacular exhibition of ice skating, which many members of the club had never before witnessed.

Although he was only seven years old at the time, Bob Jones remembers the first Southern Amateur Golf Championship he ever saw. F.G. Bird, an East Laker, was slated to win it that year, and second choice was Ellis Knowles of Pensacola, Florida, cousin of an AAC golfing member. Both men fell by the wayside, and this Amateur, played at East Lake in 1909, was finally won by a plodding golfer named Jack Adrington, from Memphis, Tennessee.

In spite of the more than 150 major trophies and medals he won, two of his cups Jones was always most proud of was his first AAC championship that he had to win three consecutive times for the prize, and a similar trophy donated by Davidson-Freeman Company of Atlanta, for AAC club competition. The account of these two cups helped to recall some of the early golfing history of the club. Here it is, as Jones told it to the author:

"One of the cups I'm proudest of is the first club championship cup I won. It was put up in 1907, with the provision that it must be won three times by the same golfer before he could retain possession of it. In 1907 and 1908 it was won by F.G. Bird, who lived in a house that faced the middle of No. 3 fairway.

"In 1909 and 1910 the cup was won by W.R. Tichenor. Dick

was a lawyer. He was a little fellow, but an Auburn football player. Mother used to know him when she spent a lot of time down at Auburn, and he was in college there at the time.

"In 1911, H.G. Scott was winner. Scotty was a northerner who came here for a while. He was a good golfer. Later I used to see him in New York where he lived at the Park Lane Hotel.

"In 1912, G.H. Atkinson was the club champion. I have a hazy recollection of Atkinson as a big, tall fellow, but never knew much about him.

"George Adair won in 1913. This, you know, was Perry Adair's father, and Perry won it the next year for the first time.

"I won it for the next three straight years and got permanent possession of the trophy. After that, I think they started giving a trophy to the winner each year. I never played in the club championship any more after that."

Bob Jones's second most cherished trophy was the Davidson-Freeman cup. Davidson-Freeman Company was a retail jeweler outfit in Atlanta and they presented the cup to the club with the same three winner provisions of the club championship.

"F.G. Bird also put his name on this trophy in 1909 and 1910," Jones recalled. "Bird also won the Southern Amateur in 1910. He was a very effective player. He had a short, little backswing and hit the ball with a sort of flip. He gave it a little twist up at the top of his finish. He was a short man and very strong, and I remember that he sported a heavy, impressive mustache.

"The next year, 1911, the Davidson-Freeman cup was won by Dick Tichenor, then in 1912 by Hamilton Block, in 1913 by T.B. Fay, who not surprisingly was always called 'Elfy'. In 1914 it was won by Veazy Rainwater, in 1915 by Perry Adair, who won it again in 1916. I won it first in 1917 and again in 1919 and 1920. There was no winner for 1918, probably because of the war. It's a beautiful trophy—one of the prettiest I've seen. Feel the weight—I'd sure hate to have to pay for it in today's silver market.

"I might add that one of the finest matches I ever had was against Richard Hickey in the finals of the Davidson-Freeman tournament. We played 36 holes without a soul watching us, and we both played fine golf. I finally beat him three and two."

Jones generally considered that his first big step toward major tournament golf was in 1915 when, at the age of 13, he won the Roebuck Country Club Invitational Tournament in Birmingham. This was the same year he conquered the Davidson-Freeman Cup event at East Lake, and both the AAC and Druid Hills Club championships. Other tournaments he won were the Cherokee Invitation at Knoxville, when he could hardly walk from an attack of lumbago; the Birmingham Invitation; East Lake Invitation; and he followed these up with his first Georgia State Amateur at Brookhaven in Atlanta in 1916.

He qualified in his first National Amateur Championship in 1916 and won his first two matches.

He won his next Southern Amateur in 1917, and since tournament golf was discontinued because of World War I, spent much of the next two years playing benefit matches for the Red Cross.

The year 1919 has been called his "runner-up" year. He finished second in the Southern Amateur, second in the Canadian Open, second in the Southern Open at his East Lake home course, and was runner-up in the U.S. Amateur.

In 1920 he won the Southern Amateur at Chattanooga, and in 1922 the Southern Amateur at East Lake and tied for second spot in the National Open. This was the last of what are known as Bob's "lean years."

The period from 1923 through 1930 is his greatest and most productive in competitive golf. He devoted himself generally to the major tournaments and piled up an impressive record which ended in his Grand Slam that has never been, and probably never will be, equalled. In 21 tries for the U.S. Amateur, U.S. Open, British Amateur and British Open, he won 13 of these and finished second in four others. Look at the score:

1923—won U.S. Open, medalist in U.S. Amateur; 1924—won U.S. Amateur, second in U.S. Open; 1925—won U.S. Amateur, second in U.S. Open; 1926—won U.S. Open, won British Open, runner-up in U.S. Amateur; 1927—won U.S. Amateur, won British Open; 1928—won U.S. Amateur, second in U.S. Open; 1929—won U.S. Open; 1930—won U.S. Amateur, won U.S. Open, won British Amateur, won British Open.

In this record are a number of noteworthy points:

For eight years Jones was either U.S. Amateur or Open Champion, culminating in the Grand Slam.

At the U.S. Amateur at Oakmont in 1925, the two golfers who met in the finals to play for the championship were Jones and Watts Gunn, both East Lakers. Never before or since have the finalists in this event been members of the same club.

Neither Jones nor Gunn, who were close friends as well as club mates, ever lost the vivid memory of that match at Oakmont. Both were playing superb golf and when they came to what Bob termed the "ghost hole" because the blast of a nearby megaphone had cost him the hole and a match with Davy Herron six years before, Gunn at 2 under par, had Jones one up in the Amateur finals, and was playing what Bob termed "the hottest inspirational golf I ever faced."

The "ghost hole" was a 600-yarder. Gunn was comfortably on

in three, but Jones' third shot found the bunker. He felt that if he lost that hole, he would never again catch Gunn. Bob blasted out of the trap to within 10 feet of the cup and sank his putt for a par to halve the hole.

"That set him on fire," Watts recalled. "Jeepers! From there in I shot the best golf I knew how to shoot, but you know what I faced? He showed me a 3–3–4–3–3–4 and at the end of the first eighteen holes I was four down. When he started the afternoon round at 4–3, it cooked my goose. I never caught up."

Most important of all Bob Jones' contributions to golf was the high integrity he brought to the game. A typical story is about the championship he once lost by calling a penalty stroke on himself. No one else saw the ball move as he addressed it in the rough, but he insisted on the penalty that cost him first place in the event. When the press commented enthusiastically on this display of honesty and sportsmanship, Jones replied, "You might as well brag on a man for *not* robbing a bank."

From his humble beginning at East Lake and all through his star-studded achievements developed Bob's great philosophy of golf, which he has so aptly summed up in a couple of now famous quotes:

"No man will ever have golf under his thumb. No round will ever be so good that it could not have been better. Perhaps that is why golf is the greatest of games. You are not playing a human adversary. You are playing a game. You are playing Old Man Par."

And:

"On the golf course, a man may be the dogged victim of inexorable fate, be struck down by an appalling stroke of tragedy, become the hero of unbelievable melodrama, or the clown in a side-splitting comedy—any of these within a few hours, and all without having to bury a corpse or repair a tangled personality."

Because of Bobby Jones the name of East Lake Country Club is known around the world, in places where the Atlanta Club had never been heard of, but he also served his club in many ways which had little to do with golfing championships. He was on AAC's Board of Dirctors from 1928 until 1947 and served as President of the club in 1946. Before, during, and after the time of these official duties, he contributed his invaluable experience to the growth and progress of the club. During and following those two decades Jones had a big voice in major decisions of policy and program, which saw many changes and important moves as the new club building on Carnegie Way, the addition of a second 18 holes at East Lake to accommodate the increase in golfing traffic, and the addition of a yacht club on Lake Lanier, a U.S. Corps of Engineers impoundment north of Atlanta and within easy access of a majority of AAC members.

Jones's shoulders were stalwart enough, but he did not have to carry East Lake's reputation as "the club of champions" all alone. Almost from the time of its creation, the Atlanta Athletic Club country club out in the wilds of DeKalb County, made its muscles felt wherever the game of golf was in competition. Many of these champions over the years were East Lake residents and practically reared on the golf course which, in spite of its numerous face-liftings, was always considered championship caliber and inspired in those budding golfers the kind of confidence that stayed with them wherever and whenever they were contestants.

One of the stories Bob Jones told was about a young fellow who was brought up in a house just behind the 4th green of the No. 2 course, which lay across Second Avenue from the East Lake original. His father and mother were golfers and like most of the boys reared around East Lake, he spent all of his spare time with a golf club in his hands.

"One afternoon," Jones recalls, "we were sitting up at the old 19th hole that used to overlook the 9th green and this youngster was playing and came along. He put his second shot over the lake, about 75 yards short of the green and pitched up about three or four feet from the hole. He had a beautiful swing, and at the table where we were sitting, someone said, 'That kid swings like a champ. Isn't it a shame that since his father and mother are so small, he'll really never grow up big enough to play championship golf.'"

The "kid" they were discussing was Charlie Yates and he did grow up more than six feet tall, muscular and proficient enough to win a lot of championships, among them the U.S. Intercollegiate, Western Amateur and British Amateur. He was also on a couple of Walker Cup teams.

Ralph McGill, Editor of the *Atlanta Constitution*, followed his townsman through those hectic days of the British Amateur and wrote from Scotland:

"Trudging along behind Charlie Yates as he marched through wind and rain and sun to win the British amateur golf championship at Troon, I found myself thinking of East Lake and its members.

"The old tradition had come alive again, and here, after a lapse of eight years, was another golfer from East Lake, bringing terror and dark days to British golf. East Lake was on the march, and I hoped the members appreciate what it means to be a member of the East Lake club, a club known wherever golf is played. Thousands were asking how one club could produce so many fine golfers, and two British amateur champions within so short a span.

"I knew how the locker room faithfuls, and the caddies and attendants, and fine George Sargent were suffering as the field grew smaller and smaller. But Yates remained at the end of each day, until at last the day came when he and East Lake were left to fight a lone battle for America.

"As long as golf is a subject of conversation, they will tell of that Friday when his eagle "two" shook Cyril Tolley, and of his really magnificent comeback to catch Hector Thompson at the eighteenth and beat him at the nineteenth with as bold and fine a putt as golf has seen. Ten thousand men and women cheered him when the putt dropped, and he looked up, a finalist.

"The next day he won the championship from a big Irishman (R.C. Ewing—3 and 2). East Lake and Atlanta had done it again."

Charlie Yates has gone on in later life to a successful business career in banking and railroading.

Watts Gunn was one of the few who, without having been born near the course or spending his early years playing golf there, brought fame to East Lake. He became a member of AAC before the mid-1920s while at Georgia Tech, and eventually served on its Board of Directors and as President of the Club in 1953–54.

Gunn was born in Macon in 1905 and attended Lanier High School there. His college was Georgia Tech and while there he developed his golf game. Here are the highlights of his golfing record:

In 1925 when he was runner-up to Bob Jones in the National Amateur, he was also East Lake champion. In 1927 he was champion in both the Southern and National Intercollegiate competitions. In 1928 he won the Southern Amateur and Southern Open championships. He was a member of the U.S. Walker Cup teams in 1926 and 1928.

Two of Gunn's most amazing rounds in a long and distinguished golfing career were reported by O.B. Keeler in the October, 1925, issue of *The American Golfer*. This was another of those incidents at Oakmont before he and Jones met in the National Amateur finals, and is dramatic enough to be worthy of record here.

Says Keeler:

"Watts had shot the first nine holes against the Western Pennsylvania champion in a sorry 42, five strokes above par, and was two down. Then he started back 5–5, each a stroke above par, and

24

Watts Gunn & Bobby Jones

lost another hole. Then, with a great chance to win the 621 yard twelfth, he had deftly steered his third shot into a trap.

"Now it was at this precise moment, as near as I can make out, that Mr. Gunn was spiritually renovated or in some other manner made over from a nervous little neophyte sputtering shots about the scene of his first big championship, into a cold, precise, grim and implacable golfing machine clicking off pars and birdies to the utter destruction of Vincent Bradford and Jess Sweetser, and later, by a sort of reversion, giving Bobby Jones the hardest run he has had in two championships.

"I recalled plainly that Watts had waded down into that trap by the twelfth green and blasted out in a shower of river sand less than a yard from the cup, and had rammed down the putt for a par and a win. And now he was off, on a record-setting spin of winning fifteen consecutive holes in a national championship.

"It is easy enough to say that Bradford played bad golf—of course he did. But starting two up through No. 12, Vincent Bradford could have shot every hole of the next 14 in absolute par, and have been hauled back to square. Watts Gunn was simply beating the card; he had twelve holes in par and three birdies; and he missed a twelve foot putt at the sixteenth in the morning; a seven footer at the fifth in the afternoon; and a ten-footer on the 253-yard eighth hole, the last of the match, for other birdies which he might as well have had, though par was good enough to win them.

"It was as perfect an exhibition of flawless, mechanical golf as ever was seen; two putts from a moderate distance for every par; never a shot off line; never an effort for a par; but always just missing—or getting—the birdies.

"'Were you scared,' I asked, 'when you started your next match with Jess Sweetser?'

"'Scared?' he said. 'I was scared stiff. I was so scared I was numb. I was glad I was numb, because it sort of kept me from suffering so much.'

"In this numb condition, Watts shot the first nine holes (against Sweetser) in par 37, and turned 3 up, and then played the last nine in 34, just as Bobby Jones had played the second nine in 34 against Sweetser in 1922. But where Bobby went in to lunch 5 down, Watts walked off the eighteenth green in the astonishing position of 7 up.

"I walked off the green with him, an arm across his sweating shoulders, and asked, 'How do you feel now?'

"'Gee,' he said, 'I'm hungry. I'm so hungry, my pants are about to fall off.'

"Then he proceeded to abate that peril, in utter defiance of my suggestion that championships 'are won on toast and tea.'

"When Watts and Jess took the first tee for the afternoon round, Watts' run from that blast out of the No. 12 had extended to 33 holes in four strokes under par, of which he had won 24 and lost only two. In the matinee round, he did not give Jess a chance,

Bobby Jones & Alexa Sterling

26

shooting every hole exactly in par except the 9th, where he ended the match with a birdie 4, for one of the most flawless exhibitions ever seen in championship golf."

The record books are full of East Lake Country Club. names, of members who figured prominently in both regional and national tournaments. In one 16 year period, East Lake golfers brought home the Georgia State championship 9 times.

The number of runnerups and near championships by AAC members and the data behind them, possibly would fill more space than the actual winners. Here, however, is the record of championships brought back to the club in approximately half a century of competition:

U.S. OPEN:
    1923, 1926, 1930—R.T. Jones, Jr.
U.S. AMATEUR:
    1924, 1925, 1927, 1928, 1930—R.T. Jones, Jr.

Postal Official, John Kirk, Louis (Casey) Jones, Postal Official

Trophies at Augusta National

Bob Jones' last foursome: August 15, 1948.
Bob Ingram, Tommy Barnes, Bobby Jones, Henry Lindner

Best Wishe
Tommy Barnes 8-9-90

28

U.S. WOMANS AMATEUR:
    1916, 1919, 1920—Alexa Stirling
BRITISH OPEN:
    1927, 1930—R.T. Jones, Jr.
BRITISH AMATEUR:
    1930—R.T. Jones, Jr.
    1938—Charles Yates
CANADIAN WOMANS AMATEUR:
    1920, 1934—Alexa Stirling
U.S. INTERCOLLEGIATE:
    1927—Watts Gunn.
    934—Charles Yates
WESTERN AMATEUR:
    1935—Charles Yates
USGA WOMANS AMATEUR:
    1916, 1919, 1920—Alexa Stirling
SOUTHERN AMATEUR:
    1910—F.G. Bird.
    1917—1920—R.T. Jones, Jr.
    1921—Perry Adair.
    1922—R.T. Jones, Jr.
    1923—Perry Adair.
    1928—Watts Gunn.
    1947, 1949—Tommy Barnes.
    1955—Charles Harrison.
SOUTHERN WOMANS AMATEUR:
    1915, 1916, 1920—Alexa Stirling.
    1922, 1924—Mrs. Helen D. Lowndes.
    1929—Margaret Maddox.
GEORGIA AMATEUR:
    1916—R.T. Jones, Jr.
    1920—C.V. Rainwater.
    1922—Perry Adair.
    1923—Watts Gunn.
    1924—C.H. Ridley.
    1927—Watts Gunn.
    1928—C.H. Black, Jr.
    1931, 1932—Charles Yates.
    1939—Dan Yates.
    1941—Tommy Barnes.

In addition there have been minor tournament wins. Seven Walker Cup teams between the years 1922 and 1938, had either one or two members from East Lake.

30

III

The Lake of East Lake

Even before its acquisition by the Atlanta Athletic Club, East Lake was rated as "good" fishing waters and at least some of those who sought recreation far out in DeKalb County (in those days) found it at the end of a long fishing pole. Early in its history there was no attempt at stocking or "managing" the lake for fish or fishing. After the dam was built to impound the flow from a dozen crystal springs, the lake received its population of fish by natural means, as have most newly created waters since the beginning of time. Herons and other wading birds, migrating from nearby waters at certain seasons of the year, brought in fish eggs on their legs to establish a number of local species as bass, bream, catfish and variety of forage fish as prey for the game species. Washed off the legs of a bird in virgin waters, these eggs hatch and eventually the fry grows into breeding individuals on their own.

In the early 1900s, some of the summer colonists spent as much time at fishing as they did enjoying golf, swimming and tennis at the newly organized country club. Bobby Jones says that the only licking he ever got from his dad was for fishing in East Lake.

Bob was not especially fond of school and after his family bought a house and moved to East Lake as year-round residents, he would occasionally wade through mud puddles on his way to school. When the teacher sent him home with wet feet, he would spend the remainder of the day at play or fishing.

One day he came home with wet feet before his father went to work and his dad, "expecting my ruse, forbade me expressly to go fishing that day, or to go near the lake."

When the Colonel went out one door, Bob left by another on his way to the lake, to a dock near the boathouse. That morning he hooked the largest fish he'd ever had on a line and in his excitement he stepped off into six feet of water at the head of the dock. Ed, the boat house attendent, pulled him out, no doubt saving him for the punishment Bob says was justly deserved.

In those days, as today, the lake was noted for its bream fishing and the bream beds were recognized as landmarks—or "lake-marks." The main competitive swimming course lay between one of the bream beds and the bridge at the upper end of the lake.

Throughout the history of the club, East Lake always had its share of anglers; some were bass enthusiasts while others devoted themselves to the other species.

Not until the 1930s was the lake actually "managed" to produce better fishing. It had been stocked for many years prior to this time and the records show that in the early thirties, from 20,000 to 30,000 fish were poured into the lake each year. There is no record of kind or size but most of these were probably fingerling bass and bream. Probably most did not survive, but enough apparently came through to provide the members with reasonably good fishing.

From the middle 1930s on, the lake was drained periodically—always with opposition from the clan of fishermen. The idea was to eliminate the overbalance of certain species, and then restock with the desired fish. These waters were then fertilized as recommended by state and federal fisheries biologists, for the maximum growth of the young fish.

Along about this time, too, rules were established for the fisherman. An example of these regulations for the protection of the members as well as the fish, were published in the May, 1939, issue of *Club Times*. They were simple enough and remained basically the same, with a few additions, over the years. These earliest "Fishing Rules For East Lake" specified that:

Fishing be restricted to club members.

No children under 15 years of age permitted to fish unless accompanied by parents. Positively no servants allowed to fish under any circumstances.

Fish limits in one day: not over 3 bass, not under 12 inches in length; not over 12 bream, not under 5 inches in length; measurements to be made from tip of nose to fork of tail.

Please wet hands to prevent scalding and carefully replace all undersized fish.

No fishing off of or around boat house.

Fishing to be restricted to either rod and reel or hook and line, and to be limited to one bass outfit or one bream outfit per person—cannot fish for bass and bream, at the same time. (The object of this restriction is to eliminate the use of set lines.)

Members are cautioned not to remove or molest turtle traps.

No gasoline motor or electrically propelled boats permitted on lake.

These rules remained generally the same during the years in which East Lake was a part of the Atlanta Athletic Club complex. Those modifications noted over the seasons were in keeping with the changing times. One of the latest sets of fishing rules warned against fishing without a state license and the possession of a membership card as well, so that trespassers could be checked. Some added regulations were:

No swimming in the lake permitted. (This was put into effect after the construction of the Olympic swimming pool between the clubhouse and old swimming beach.)

Members were requested to keep their boats in good repair and to have life preservers or cushions aboard for safety.

Fishermen were asked not to throw bottles, cans, cartons or other debris into the water or along the shore.

Gasoline motors were still banned, but electric motors permitted.

As fishing improved the bass limit was raised to 8, with a size limit of 10 inches, and the angler was allowed 35 bream a day with no size limit. Channel catfish were added to the list with a limit of 7, not under 12 inches in length.

In later years the lake was turned over to the Game and Fish Commission for management on a scientific basis and was drained, seined and restocked perodically every few years. This draining was done in the fall after the swimming period was past. The lake was kept fertilized according to recommended practices. This treatment of fishing waters was not without complaint by the angling members, many of whom insisted that the longer the lake was left undisturbed, the more and larger fish it would produce.

That proper management paid off, however, is in evidence time and again throughout the scanty records, which reveal quite a number of lunker largemouth bass taken out of the lake. One of the first of these records show a 7 pounder taken by Dozier Lowndes, who appropriately was Chairman of the Fish Committee. The largest recorded bass was a 10 pound 4 ounce monster caught by Walter N. Pendleton in March, 1948. Both before and after that date, a surprisingly large number of largemouths over 6 pounds were caught in the 27 acre lake. There is no written information on the incredible strings of bream in the old days or of bream and catfish produced by these fertile waters in later years.

East Lake was popular as a family club, and that the lake itself was one of the most enjoyed facilities at the country club for over half a century is on record throughout the literature of AAC. Common practice was for a golfer to bring his family to the lake where they might enjoy the beach and other activities while he slugged it out with his partners or with old man par. Later they might get together again for dinner in the main club room or on the dining terrace.

While the fisherman had their own set of do-and-don'ts which did not allow invading or disturbing the swimming beach, the swimmer also provided their rules, which were set up for the safety and pleasure of all. An example of these regulations appear in an early issue of *Club Times*. They provided that members and guests bathing in the lake must change clothes in the bath house (where the lockers and showers were located) and must not appear in bathing suits elsewhere than on the beach.

There was a charge for nonmember guests of 50¢ on week days and $1 on week ends and holidays and a heavy fine for not registering guests. Wives or unmarried daughters of members were not allowed male guests who lived within a radius of 40 miles of Atlanta.

Other rules specified no alcoholic beverages served or consumed on the lawn or lake front; no one permitted in the lake except when life guard was on duty; no swimming after 7 p.m.; swimming authorized in the regular designated areas only; no tubes or floats permitted beyond the ropes (which outlined the swimming area); no golf clubs, footballs or softballs allowed near the beach; no pets permitted on the beach; no food allowed in the swimming area; no boating or surf-boarding in the swimming area; waterfront activities from 10 a.m. to 7 p.m. only.

Special efforts were made at the lake to provide pleasure for the entire family. A "Sport Short" in July 1938 by Fred Lanoue, AAC athletic coach and swimming instructor, says that "use of the water front is increasing daily due to the installation of new equipment suitable for young and old. There were two regulation diving boards on the large raft for members and guests, and a small one on the small raft for children. A new piece of floating equipment called a 'swinging jigaboo' proved itself very popular.

"A badminton court has been laid out on the lawn and also a croquet course. A new game 'tetherball' has been going steadily with children waiting their turns. A ping-pong table has been installed in the new recreation room below the bathhouse locker rooms. There is also a revival of interest in horseshoes and plans are being made for a tournament. A sand box has been put in to

Behind the Scenes
Mack Tomlinson, Jack Rollins, Morris Durrett

Robert Tyre Jones
1902–1971

Past Presidents   W G Kallenberg, L H (Casey) Jones,
Toby Sexton, Harvey Robertson, Dr Charles Allard.
(missing: Dave Heinsma)

Paul R. Grigsby

keep the smaller children happy. Acrobatics and gymnastic stunts are enjoyed most any pleasant afternoon, using mats to safeguard the children."

The waterfront at East Lake apparently was a busy place!

Times were changing: 1938 was the year in which the bathing suit was modified so that men could go swimming in the lake without having to wear the tops to their bathing suits!

In addition to promoting games and contests, Lanoue perennially came up with something new in the way of entertainment for the pleasure of his members. A special feature reported in the summer issue of *Club Times* drew a sizable contingent of AAC members to see the "water magicians demonstrating their act" in the premier outdoor show of the season. Here are some of the acts the members looked forward to seeing:

"Jack Carver will be tied fast to a chair and tossed into the water with arms pinioned to his sides. We hope he comes up right side up. Alvin Vaughan, Jr., otherwise known as "Jerry the Gristleman" will be forced to exert all his great strength to do his stunt, which is tow a rowboat with six passengers while his hands and feet are tied. George Hiles will defy the laws of common sense and swim all over the place with feet tied tightly and hands tied tightly behind his back.

"Clyde Carver, locally known as 'Catfish Charlie' because of his propensity for looking on the bottom, will attempt to break the existing world's record for staying underwater for 6 minutes, 35 seconds. In a recent practice, Catfish Charlie stayed below 5 minutes, 45 seconds with no trouble at all.

"We are very fortunate in having the services of Achemed Abdullah, the Bohemian champion who has invented a startling new stroke which shoots him over the water at an unbelieveable rate. Achmed recently beat two expert paddlers in a canoe. He will race the best local swimmer obtainable.

"John Hiles will drink a whole bottle of Coca-Cola underwater and if you don't think that's a stunt, just try it. Bob Roberts will also eat a banana underwater, he says he could eat a whole bunch, but we're holding him to one. From the sublime to the ridiculous, Biljim Yelding, height 9 feet 2 inches, will race Charlie Smith, height 24 inches.

"The management is sparing no expense in an effort to get 'The Great Oliver' to perform his mystifying escape act. With feet tightly bound and bona fide handcuffs on his writsts, Oliver is put in a canvas bag with a large rock, the top is tightly tied and Oliver is cast into the deep. Strong men blanch at this feat.

"Besides an exhibition of fancy diving and canoe races, there will be a comedy skit depicting the 'heathen Chinese' saving lives, also a formation canoe drill.

"The show starts at 3:00 and its going to be pretty crowded, so come early and bring coats and sweaters, because some of the tricks will produce a bumper crop of cold chills."

It sure sounds like it might have been fun!

The fisherman, boaters and bathers lived amicably together over many decades. Then in the 1950s, with the growing number of AAC members and with the expanding management of the lake for fishing, conflicts began to develop. The beach was becoming overcrowded and the pavilion locker room facilities somewhat cramped. Fertilizing the lake for fish was the cause for some consternation among the ladies who claimed that the algae "bloom" created by the chemicals splotched and ruined their swim suits. The sanitary people conceded that the spring fed lake was not as clean and unpolluted as once it was when fewer swimmers used it, and there was no way to treat the pollution over the entire lake.

In late 1957 the AAC Board of Directors announced that to solve these problems, a new swimming pool complex would be built at East Lake, between the men's locker room and beach which had been so many decades of use. The pool, designed by J. Wylly Keck, Jr. and Associates of Atlanta, with Tony Shennan and Associates of Miami, includes all facilities and modern equipment to the tune of $150,000. Specifications were given for the project, which was declared the largest club pool in the city and one of the finest anywhere.

"- a T-shape pool, being 164 feet 2 inches in its longest dimension (i.e., over half the length of the playing area of a football field), the (combined) width of the big and little pool is 42 feet. The largest distance across the width of the pool (at the T) is 82 feet, 2 inches from the diving boards to the far side. The depth of the large pool will be from 3 feet to 12 feet in the diving area under the boards. The (adjacent) wading pool is 20 feet square with a sprinkler in the center and in 6 to 12 inches in depth."

The bathhouse and snack bar were built between the pool and parking lot, with men's and women's locker rooms on opposite sides of the building, which also housed a filtering plant. Extending from the snack bar along and beyond the length of the pool was a grass terrace with tables, chairs and umbrellas.

Special equipment included underwater lights and a sprinkler system to help cool the water in the pool.

The lake was closed to all but fishing and boating, but the old beach below the pool terrace was left for the children to play on under the supervision of their parents.

The pool was opened in the June of the next year and drew an even larger number of swimmers than had used the lake the summer before. The records showed upward of 500 persons a day enjoying the new facility. Immediately, classes of swimming instruction were set up and intra-city swimming meets scheduled with other clubs around Atlanta.

The old club house on the lake, which had stood before the country club came into existence, and which was East Lake headquarters before the first club house was built, was removed and the dock facilities improved for the boaters and fishermen. The new pool swim rules remained practically the same as those that had applied to the lake.

The new pool complex brought an end to an era and turned East Lake over to the anglers and boaters for the first time in its history.

IV

The Club Houses Over the Years

East Lake was struck by two disastrous fires. The main club house, built in 1907, burned to the ground in 1912. Before the ashes cooled, AAC officers were planning a larger, more attractive and more serviceable building in the same location. Records show that architects for the new club house were Hentz and Reid, who, plausibly enough, made this notation on the contract - "It is the intention to build as much of the building of fireproof construction as possible."

R.M. Walker was the builder, and sub-contracts were let with C.W. Baxter "to put in a complete plumbing system, including 4 showers, a 'water closet' urinal, a lavoratory and toilet off the golf instruction room, and a urinal in the men's general toilet on the second floor," all for the sum of $2,940.00.

At the same time (July, 1914) McGaughey Electric Company signed a contract for a complete electric and telephone system for $1,700.

The Directors of that day found themselves with one of the many problems that faced the club's slate of officers over three-quarters of a century. The insurance, which had seemed adequate when the first club building was erected in 1907 and was sufficient to cover that building then, was now not enough. Atlanta was growing rapidly, and over as short a period as half a dozen years, building material and labor had risen substantially. Added to this fact was a growing club with an increasing number of golfers, swimmers, tennis players and others who had found the country club a delightful playground except for the most inclement weeks of the year. This called for a larger building and expanded facilities. This, with the rising costs, left the club with a deficit even larger than its officers had anticipated.

Several of the usual courses to absorb this loss were open. The Directors must either make a substantial assessment, raise the dues to an unprecedented amount, or fantastically increase the service fees, plus putting new charges on the use of those facilities which, heretofore, had been free. Any of those alternatives could mean a loss of membership, make the club less attractive for new members or curtail the use of facilities by those who resented the higher prices and added fees.

As one might imagine, this problem evoked long and serious discussion. It was finally solved in 1915 by the issuance of 25-year 6-percent gold bonds, with interest and principal to be paid in gold coin. As collateral, AAC gave a First Mortgage on all club properties.

This rebuilt clubhouse stood for more than a dozen years before it, too, was destroyed by fire in 1926. For a second time, AAC went for larger quarters and expanded facilities. This one was an English Tudor style clubhouse of three stories, with more dining space and a men's large locker room on the second floor. This building, still magnificent as it stands today, was gradually enlarged and improved over the years.

In the 1940s, the open air dining terrace at East Lake was enclosed and the men's locker room moved from the second to the ground floor. This new rectangular wing, 100 by 160 feet, designed by architects Stevens and Wilkerson, and built by J.A. Jones Construction Co., provided for a luxurient carpeted locker room with two sets of showers and 820 lockers, with the golf shop and the men's grill located adjacent to the locker room. The top of all this was a full concrete terrace just off the upstairs dining room. This open terrace, landscaped with potted plants, overlooked the lake, and later, a swimming pool, and from it almost all of the old golf course was visible. For many years it was the scene of Saturday

night and holiday dances held under the stars, and special Sunday buffets that usually overflowed the main dining room to the terrace.

The 1926 fire destroyed the first Bobby Jones U.S. Amateur trophy on exhibition in the main lobby. The U.S.G.A. further honored Jones by replacing the silver trophy with a solid gold replica.

"That fire burned up my golf clubs too," Jones once said with a grin, "but the U.S.G.A. evidently didn't hear about that because they failed to give me a new set of gold clubs."

By the late 1920s, the number of golfers at East Lake had increased to the point where the original golfing layout around the lake was overcrowded in good playing weather, and especially on weekends and holidays. For a year or more, dissatisfaction had been expressed by the golfing members, who finally took it upon themselves to see what could be done about it.

Across Second Avenue from the main club property lay a large undeveloped tract. Generally located between Glenwood Avenue and Memorial Drive, it was rolling terrain with a creek streaking through it. Most of it was covered with mature mixed hardwood and pine timber. The buffer zone between Second Avenue and this tract was a row of houses and building lots, one of which belonged to P.D. Yates, who had been an active member of AAC since 1901.

The Board of Directors and members were about equally divided on the purchase of this property, with the golfing contingent pushing it. The hassle went on for months. One of those who disagreed with buying urban acreage for a second golf course was club president Scott Hudson. At that time, the second East Lake clubhouse had been lost to fire, plans were underway to move the downtown club and Mr. Hudson considered it unwise to go further into debt. When the Number 2 golf course issue came up, in spite of the popular demand for this expansion, he had the courage to vote against it all of the way.

When the majority carried, however, President Hudson pitched in to do more than his share in the purchase and development of this property toward one of the city's finest courses. Later on, he gave the club a sizeable tract of land adjoining the No. 2 course he had opposed.

Donald Ross was employed as golf architect to lay out the course and did one of his spectacular jobs on the forested, rolling terrain. Fairways were cut through the woods, where enough of the huge trees were retained to give the course character and dignity. Greens were located at the most strategic spots to fit into the contours of the hillsides. A lake was planned along the creek for a later date, but was never built.

Number 4 green and number 1 tee were reasonably adjacent to the P.D. Yates home on Second Avenue, and his boys, as had Bobby Jones twenty years before them, had the run of the golf course. All developed into fine players and tournament winners, the most notable being Charlie Yates, who won the British Amateur in 1938.

Two men on whose shoulders rested a large portion of the responsibility for the development and growth during those years, served the longest terms as officers of AAC than any two other persons in the history of the club. These were Colonel Robert P. Jones, Director from 1908 to 1946, and in that long tenure of service, was President from 1937 until 1942; and Scott Hudson, who was either a Director or President from 1915 until 1946. For 18 of those 31 years he was President of AAC, during one of the club's most difficult periods, and yet, one in which, except for the lowest point in the depression years of the early 1930s, the club never ceased to grow. Scott Hudson was the man largely responsible for keeping the club alive and guiding its destinies.

Many members believed then, and today most of the old timers who knew him and were familiar with his devotion to AAC, will agree that Scott Hudson contributed much of the wisdom and business acumen that carried AAC over some of its most trying years of adversity, before and during the depression that gripped a nation.

Hudson was a colorful and fascinating personality. He was born in Danville, Kentucky in 1870 and did not come south to make Georgia his permanent home until he was 36 years old. Five years later he became a member of AAC, and was first elected to the Board of Directors in 1915, and, as its President in 1919. Here is what they said about him at a testimonial dinner given when he retired as President to take over the Chairmanship of the Board in 1937:

"In the face of stern demands made by a material world, it is well that a Divine Providence inspires some men of great capabilities with a spirit of unselfishness and a willingness to give of themselves and their time for the benefit of their fellow men. Fortunate indeed is that group of people who find in their midst a man of such character and capacity. Their lives and their progress become richer and happier by virtue of his association with them.

"Sixty seven years have sprinkled with strands of grey the little red head which first saw the light of day at Danville, Kentucky, on March 27, 1870. But that little red head was destined to illuminate old trails and blaze new ones in the years ahead.

"His father, Lynn Hudson, was a mule breeder, buyer and

trader between Danville, Kentucky, and New Orleans. Center College at Danville polished the red headed Scott and made him a member of Phi Delta Theta fraternity, but his real education came from his dad, who knew mules and horses.

"So it is that we pass lightly over the intervening years until at the age of twenty two we find our hero driving the mare, "Mattie H" to his first winning race in the field where later he was to become a national figure. From 1894 to 1903 he flashed around the Grand National Circuit, probably the greatest trainer and driver the Circuit ever knew."

Even so, that does not tell the whole story. Scott Hudson was one of the noted sports personalities of his time. It was only natural that being a Blue Grass Kentuckian and having a mule trader for a daddy, that his early interest should be in horses, and that he went the route of harness racing, both as a trainer and competitor. His most noted and profitable years on the track were 1901–2 and 3, when he followed the Grand Circuit much as golfers follow the "tour" of today. He was in demand both as a trainer and driver.

Two of the most widely acclaimed events in which he participated got reams of newspaper space all over America. His greatest day at the track was on July 15, 1902, when he swept the field, winning all four races, each with a different horse. His purse for this day's work brought him $40,000 and was equivalent to a "grand slam" in golf. It has never been equalled in the history of the sport.

Young Hudson's second, and practically as great an accomplishment, was racing a blind horse he had trained and with steady, sure reins, driving his charge to victory over a field of other notable horses. The name "Rhythmic" still stands after more than three quarters of a century as a monument to the colossal skill of the man. Blind Rhythmic went on to become one of the big money winners in the Hudson stable, but the drama of that first win inspired a classic bit of verse by poetess Ella Wheeler Wilcox. For more than 70 years it has been quoted and requoted and here deserves recognition as a part of the Hudson biography.

> The record was this when the race was done -
> The Great Blind Conqueror Rhythmic won.
>
> He sped through the dark though the sun rose high
> In the cloudless arch of an August sky.
>
> The world for him was a ball of black,
> But he heard his master, he felt the track,
> He trusted the hands on the reins, he knew
> That the one on the whip was Love's hand, too.

He saw not the path where his feet must fall;
To the eyes of his driver he trusted all.

Faith and courage and strength and speed,
They won the day for the brave, blind steed.

Great is the lesson, O mortal blind,
God is the Master, His whip is kind.

Trust in His purpose, though lost in night
The hand of the Driver will guide aright;
Courage and faith and an even pace
And God's eyes guarding will win the race.
Ella Wheeler Wilcox

Hudson gave up racing and disposed of most of his equine interests in 1904. For a while he and his wife traveled, and in 1906 they moved to Atlanta to establish a business. Most hauling and delivering as well as human conveyance was by horses and mules and Mr. Hudson set up an elaborate livery stable just off Marietta Street west of the city. He trafficked in stock and ran a rental service of drays, wagons and carriages—a sort of you-drive-it system of its day.

He loved animals, and when he got out of the horse training business, Hudson switched much of his affection to bird dogs, which over many seasons he bred and trained. His dogs won consistently in field trials from local to national championships, and one of them, McTyre, sold for an unprecedented sum of $7,500. For years Hudson was President of the Georgia Field Trial Association.

Although he ran his own business and served on many other Boards of Directors, Scott Hudson was never too busy to follow outdoor activities. In 1911 he joined the Atlanta Athletic Club. He was approaching middle age when he took up golf to become a much better than average golfer for those days. He shot a 79 over the East Lake course to qualify for the Southern Amateur.

His personality, business philosophy and financial shrewdness made him a logical choice in 1915 for AAC's Board of Directors, and this eventually proved one of the lucky stars in AAC's crown. He was on the Board for four years and then elected President of the Club, a position he held from 1919 until 1937, when he relinquished the reins to Colonel Bob Jones.

It was only fitting that one of our most noted athletes should hold the club presidency longer than any other man. Not only that, but the club was fortunate that a man of Scott Hudson's devotion and leadership should be at the helm to guide the club through its progressive, as well as its most troublesome years.

There is little record of those first few years Mr. Hudson served as club President. Generally it is known that the membership was growing and in the early and middle 1920s, the chief executive and his Board handled the establishment at East Lake and on Auburn Avenue in such a manner that each well-run place showed a sizeable profit.

The lean years started when the East Lake clubhouse was gutted by fire for a second time. The Board was in the process of converting the Art Theatre into a new downhome home. Acquisition of land for the second 18-hole golf course was underway. Right in the middle of all this the "great depression" of 1929 struck. Banks closed. Stock market traders jumped out of tall buildings. U.S. business came virtually to a standstill. The country was in a fair way of going broke. In the midst of all this, AAC found itself with new properties, a decreasing membership, almost $1 million in debt. It was hard put to pay its managers and other personnel.

Scott Hudson gave up everything else and devoted himself to the management of the club. Buying and remodeling a new downtown club building, rebuilding East Lake with its new golf course had practically depleted the bank account and put the borrowing of fresh money on a hazardous basis.

Hudson became a fulltime working president. With no funds to employ high priced executives, he ran the establishment himself, with the help of young men of recognized ability, either recently out of college, or who were unhappy with their job or situation and were looking for a change.

The President knew how necessary it was to gear his organization to the times. He once wrote that—"In the operation of a club, as in the operation of a business, it is necessary from time to time to meet new conditions that arise. Not only are club changes required in management, but also in the method of securing desirable new members.

"The Atlanta Athletic Club has consistently aimed at better management, better membership and better service. In fact it has been a leader in most progressive club activities, particularly in competitive sports and in the provision of excellent facilities for the recreation and diversion of members—benefits enjoyed only through the cooperative action which is the basis of club existence."

Apparently with this in mind, Hudson employed young men

and developed them into the managers and other top personnel which kept AAC going through many of those years after the club had passed from his leadership on to other hands.

According to A.S. Hapholdt, one of those assistants, Mr. Hudson lived on East Lake Drive, close to the club. There wasn't money to hire a greens superintendent or high priced labor, so he took the job of course supervision, on himself.

The man Mr. Hudson employed to keep the course in shape was J.O. Parker, a local farmer who knew little about greens and fairways and probably cared less, but was well acquainted with the problems of working laborers and mules.

One item of equipment in those days was the swamp cane, or local bamboo. Those with brushy tops were cut out of the cane thickets along the creek below East Lake, and tied together as brooms. These were used to sweep the greens after they had been mowed.

Almost every morning, shortly after daylight, Hudson went to the maintenance shops to leave instructions with his wage hands on cutting, fertilizing and other golf course work. He arrived in his office at the downtown club by 8:00 o'clock to take up the day's business there, *after* planning the day's work at East Lake. As a labor saving device on the course, Mr. Hudson was said to have invented the rotary hoe. His conception was a barrel, with 40-penny nails driven through from the inside. The barrel was weighted with rocks to spike the fairways as well as the greens.

The President cut all corners. Hapholdt, who was the downtown club manager, got up between 4:00 and 5:00 o'clock and drove to the farmers market out on Central Avenue, to shop for vegetables and other rations at a reduced price. Almost every morning he would come to the club with his back seat and car running boards loaded down with boxes and bags of vegetables and other truck. Once in a great while he would wait until Mr. Hudson came in before 8:00 o'clock to go with him, to visit with many of the farmers he had known through the horse and mule trade.

One of the little known stories told about Mr. Hudson's thoroughness in running his club and watching expenses, concerned towels. One morning he was on his way between his home on East Lake Drive and the downtown office. One of his neighbors, who was a club member, lived just around the corner. On the clothes line in his neighbors back yard hung seven large bath towels from the East Lake locker room, identified by the large letters EAST LAKE printed on a red strip through the center of the towel.

The President went straight to his downtown office, wrote a

letter to his friend and neighbor, advising him that he was, as of that moment, suspended as a member of the Atlanta Athletic Club,and that his suspension would remain in effect until he returned those seven towels to East Lake.

The depression grew worse in the early 1930s. Money was a scarce commodity. Other athletic clubs fell by the wayside. AAC's members began to cash in their $100 certificates and resign. In those dark days the membership dropped from 1,250 to less than 500. Those who could afford the nominal dues of $7 a month usually had pocketbooks too lean to allow for parties or entertainment or eating anywhere except at home and the use of the club dropped alarmingly. The best solution to this seemed to be more members. This was a life or death matter, and all remaining members got into the act as "spark plugs" with Lew Gordon as Spark Plug Chairman, and Alva Maxwell leading the Glad Hand Committee. The club literally pulled itself up by its boot straps, with every man a salesman. It was an extraordinary and superb job and the rolls went up again, slowly at first and with increasing vigor. Before the depression years wore themselves out, the membership strength was practically back to normal.

During this low period Scott Hudson ran the club like a working manager. He was there every morning for a full eight or nine hours. Excerpts from some of his letters indicate that he attended to even the minute details:

"Dear Bill: From the reports I have gotten recently, your son, Will, has been giving Mr. Bell considerable trouble at East Lake. On the 27th he was over at the Club with young John ———, running all over the building and not stopping until they had gone into the attic where we keep our sprinkler system, which they were likely to trip and flood the whole building.

"I feel sure that you do not approve of this, and while Bill, Jr. is a Junior member, I do not like for the Board of Directors to handle him, and feel it would be more appropriate for you to do this. I would suggest that you stop him from the use of both clubs for at least 30 days.

"I feel that you will cooperate with us and know you will receive this letter as it is written, and with kindest regards . . ."

"Dear Dr. Hopping: On my return home I found yours of September 13th together with your application. This application will be passed on by the Membership Committee at once at their first meeting.

"In regard to the rooms at the Club, will say that the monthly rate is from $50 to $75 per room for one person. These are all outside rooms with both tub and shower baths, running ice water

and free telephone service. They are nicely furnished and have been very popular with our members. The meals here too are very reasonable as one can live here for $110 a month for both room and board. That is the meals on the a la carte so that you can pay for the meals you get, which in case you are away, makes the price even more reasonable.

"You will be notified in the next few days, and in the meantime if you will drop by the Club I will be glad to show you through the building and let you select a room if you so desire."

"Dear Mr. George: It gives me pleasure to notify you that I have placed you on the Fish Committee, your Chairman being Mr. A.C. Plage. Hoping you will accept this appointment and with kindest regards . . ."

"Gentlemen: Mr. Al Dunn of this city spoke to me the other day about receiving quotations from you on Kentucky hams, smoked and cured, at 28¢.

"If you will express to the Atlanta Athletic Club two of these hams for sample, sending us bill for same, will be glad to take it up with you in case they are satisfactory. Would like also to know the amount you can furnish in case they are satisfactory."

One of the requirements for bringing the club through both

the high and low years must have been a sense of humor. Scott Hudson was endowed to a high degree with that quality, and it was one facet of his character that made those working with him and under him, devoted to the "boss." One example of that humor was in a report Mr. Hudson gave to the AAC members in 1940, as Chairman of the Board after his long term as President.

"Under the "New Deal" management, conditions at both the City and Country clubs have been vastly improved. No doubt this was largely caused by a more vigorous policy of trying to make the best of it all. It has been the custom of the club's officers to worry too much. Under the New Deal policy 97-percent of our officers have cut their fretting down to 87½-percent for the fiscal year.

"Your club was able to get a little work done at both branches, by the appointment of a few committees, thus saving the executives a major amount of their time for their own pleasures. These committees are to be complimented on their work. The Golf Committee, with its sub-committees, numbering eleven, have done a fine job.

"The Greens Committee has found it necessary to appoint sub-committees on each variety of grass. The committees are making a thorough and complete investigation, and hope in a few years to furnish you with greens that you can write home about.

"There is also a committee on fairways. It is working overtime taking in damn near all the rough, so the Rough Committee is now complaining about having nothing to do.

"The Committee on Traps has been closing those in their way and digging new ones to catch the other fellow.

"The Committee on Bridges has done a neat job of decorating.

"The Fish Committee contemplates building two more lakes and a hatchery, and has a vague idea of ultimately supplying good fishing.

"The Woman's Golf Committee has been successful in taking charge of the No. 1 course on Sunday afternoons.

"We found that the Tennis Committee was being overworked, and deciding it was necessary to relieve them of some of their duties, created the Racket Committee.

"The Towel Committee has recommended that new towels be used exclusively, thereby saving laundry bill.

"The Pencil Committee has insisted that all pencils be cut in two and that only one shall be allowed to a foursome, which they say would result in a saving of 87-percent, or about $1.93 for the year.

"The Management had expected to name several other committees for East Lake, but the lack of meeting space was a question.

However, since the Greens Committee has motorized all equipment and the barn has been left vacant, I understand your Management expects to remodel it, installing electric lights, and assigning the various stalls to committee chairmen for offices, and to assure a full attendance at each meeting, to give them free food, this food to consist of the greens clippings, and in case of snow, bran mash and baled hay.

"As for the Town Club, the committees have been functioning to perfection. The Membership Committee and Athletic Committee, the Glad Hand Committee, the Entertainment Committee, the Racket Committee, and the Swimming Committee, have all been working over-time, and since the wage and hours bill has come into effect, the Management contemplates the appointing of several other committees as soon as the New Member Committee will furnish them with material.

"The first of these new committees will be most important, the one on taxes. It will be necessary for this committee to have several sub-committees. Two for the Federal Government, one for the state, five for the county, and two for the city; a committee on purchases, with complete instructions not to buy from anyone except a club member or his friends, and in no case to pay more than double value. A Committee on Sales, to see that no Club member or his guest pay over 50-percent of the regular price of any article. And in case a member is not satisfied, for the Committee to give it to him and pay for it themselves.

"The Management also contemplates utilizing the entire rear wall of the City Club for listing those committeemen. This free advertising will be their compensation.

"The general outlook is good. This club will continue to pay its regular dividend, which is twice the amount you can get at any other club at any price.

"In case a club member has any grievance, or wishes to make any suggestion, *don't* burden any committee. Take it up direct with the President."

"Time and space being limited, I have only mentioned a few of the most important committees. No mention has been made of the Frog Committee, Rat Committee or Sewer Committee, all of which I am Chairman. I will report all frogs scarce, rats plentiful and sewers stopped."

When Mr. Hudson made this report as Chairman of the Board, Colonel Robert P. Jones, Bobby's father, had succeeded him as President, in 1937. After 30 years as one of its Directors, Colonel Bob knew as much about his club as any other man. Some who remember the Colonel describe him as one of the most colorful and intriguing personalities ever associated with, or one who devoted himself so assiduously to the welfare of AAC. While big Bob Jones was not a charter member, his association was practically for the life of the club until the time of his death. He joined in 1902, the year his to-be-famous son Bobby was born, and had a big hand in the development of the East Lake property. In another chapter we told the story of how he was one of the early summer residents and later a prominent citizen in the East Lake community and of his influence on the ultimate successful career of his son.

Many stories were told about Colonel Bob Jones. His golf swing, except on the practice tee, was terrible. One day in the clubhouse, he showed his swing to his son Bob, and asked, "Son, what's the matter with that swing?" "Nothing," said Bob. "Why don't you use it sometime?"

For the forty years he served as an officer, no one could recall a Board meeting that was dull or listless when Colonel Bob was present. One of his great attributes, they said was a knack of reaching down into the middle of a maize of complicated facts and coming up with a single answer.

Colonel Bob loved a good story on himself, whether he or someone else was telling it and one of those he enjoyed most was about what he called his "most unusual tournament."

This was an intra-club tournament held between the golfers of East Lake and those of another club in a town near Atlanta. The other club contained a golfer who was every bit as proficient in the use of profanity as the Colonel, so the tournament committee arranged to pair these two against one another in the same foursome. It was agreed among the intra-club committeemen that both the Colonel and his opponent would be told the same story—that he was playing against a preacher and to keep from embarrassing his club, it would be necessary that he watch his language during the round.

Everyone who was in on the joke declared that it was probably the most hilarious round of golf ever played. When one of the contestants missed a shot—which was often—instead of going into his usual verbal barrage which had to do with the slings and arrows of outrageous fortune, he would turn red in the face, controlling his temper with obvious effort. This went on for fourteen holes, with the other members of the foursome and the gallery scarcely able to contain their own hilarity.

On the 15th hole, the Colonel's opponent missed a short putt. As he stooped over to pick up his ball on the edge of the cup, he said under his breath, "goddammedsonofabitch!" The foursome froze for an instant and Colonel Bob, only a step away, reached over and caught the man by the arm.

"What did you say?" he asked.

"Why it was nothing—nothing," the golfer stammered. The Colonel was persistent.

"What did you *say?*" he demanded.

His opponent faced him, red to the tips of his ears.

"Look, preacher," he apologized, "I couldn't help it. It just slipped out. I'm sorry."

"Preacher?" Colonel Bob roared. "Who's a preacher?"

"They told me you were," the man mumbled, and the two studied one another, the light beginning to dawn.

Those who followed the match later declared that the air was blue from that point on to the clubhouse.

In more serious matters, Colonel Bob Jones followed well for five years in the footsteps of Scott Hudson. He turned the reins over to Henry Heinz and went back to the Board for four more years before he retired.

V

Tournaments

The Golden Anniversary of the Woman's National Golf Tournament, played at East Lake on September 11–16, 1950, marked the first time a U.S.G.A. National Tournament was ever played in Atlanta. According to records, it was brought to East Lake largely through the efforts of Mrs. W.D. (Mattie) Tumlin, a long time member of the club, one of its most ardent golfers and prominent in golfing affairs around Atlanta.

The trophy awarded the winner of the U.S.G.A. affair was an artfully decorated vase of Etruscan design, presented to the U.S.G.A. in 1896 by Robert Cox of Edinburgh, Scotland, to be held by the winner for a year. The names on the cup included those of two Atlantans, Alexa Stirling (who won it three times) and Louise Suggs. In 1950, the defending champion was Mrs. Mark A. Porter, of Philadelphia. Bob Jones was honorary General Chairman of the Committee.

Bert Prather's report in the *Atlanta Constitution* might be classed as an understatement when he said:

"The Golden Anniversary Woman's National Golf Championship passed into history late Saturday afternoon when tall Bev Hanson stepped up to receive the coveted championship trophy from U.S.G.A. President James D. Standish, Jr., but sports fans and participants alike will be discussing this one for months to come.

In many ways this tournament was one of the very best in the 50-year history. Visiting U.S.G.A. officials and writers all agreed that East Lake could not have improved on its role of hosting this big tournament.

Then the tournament itself produced more than the usual run of good golf. The record-breaking 27-hole match staged between pert little Mae Murray and Uruguay's Fay Crocker was a masterful exhibition by two of the gamest battlers in Women's golf. This match may remain in the record books a long time.

The story of the extra length match mentioned by Prather was told more graphically in a plaque erected after the tournament, in the historic old East Lake Clubhouse, to commemorate the "Longest extra hole match between Miss Mae Murray of Rutland, Vermont, and Miss Fay Crocker of Montevideo, Uruguay. The match was scheduled for 18 holes. In the fourth round on Wednesday afternoon, September 13, 1950, the players were all square after 24 holes, when darkness stopped play. They resumed play next day at noon, and Miss Murray won on the 27th hole. The nine extra holes were three more than the previous U.S.G.A. Championship record.

The second notable event at East Lake was the 15th biennial British-American Ryder Cup Golf Matches played October 8–13, 1963, over the No. 1 course. In preparation for the matches, the home course went through a face lifting for three years, during which most of the old course was rebuilt and many of the holes changed to provide the quality of championship layout the tournament merited for this event. The improvements were made by Mel Warnecke, course superintendent, under the direction of George Cobb, noted golf course architect.

One of the marked improvements was in the reconstruction of the greens, which had always been blanketed with Bermuda grass in the summer months and rye in the winter—then the favorite covers of most southern golf courses. All greens were enlarged to championship size, underlaid with drainage tile and crushed stone, soil and top soil and sodded with Bent grass, all with an adequate built-in sprinkler system. Most bunkers were enlarged and 30 more added, to tighten up the course and make accuracy a premium.

All holes were improved in one way or another. An example was No. 6, known as the "island hole." This par 3 challenger was developed into one of the most beautiful holes on any course and later proved to be a favorite with the tournament players. It lay along and at a slight angle to the lake shore, with the tee overlooking the green from the hillside and the putting surface and traps occupying a goodly portion of the island, which was surrounded by a 20-foot-wide slough, with walkways to and from the green.

To increase the handicap on No. 6, the tee was extended to give the hole a playing distance of 180 yards. The slough in front of the green was widened and the bank bordering it cut down for a better view of the putting surface. The ragged ditch paralleling the slough was piped, filled and sloped to a rolling contour at the water's edge. The new green was made into a clover-leaf, guarded by traps on the left front, right and back. The surrounding slough, which was a part of the main lake, was raised by some 8 inches and made into a flowing stream by bringing in water from the upper lake, which was higher than the main lake.

The U.S. Ryder Cup team was said to be one of the strongest of all time, with 5 of its members having previously represented their country in the matches. It included Arnold Palmer, Captain, whose name was a household word in and out of golf circles; Billy Casper, Jr., one of the top players on the circuit; "Champagne" Tony Lema; Gene Littler a current top money winner; Dave Ragen, Jr., a youngster who had finished second to Jack Nicklaus in the 1963 PGA Championship; Julius Boros, an old timer who had won his share of the big tournaments; Dow Finsterwald, who had been a member of every Ryder Cup team since 1957; Billy Maxwell, who was U.S. Amateur Champion in 1951 at the age of 22; Johnny Pott, at 27 the youngest member of the team; and Bob Goalby, said to be one of the finest all-round athletes in the ranks of professional golf. Bob Rosburg was first alternate.

You already know that the Ryder Cup Matches were originated in England by Samuel Ryder, who did not start playing golf until he was past his fiftieth birthday, but became a disciple of the game.

He conceived the idea of international competition between the best players in Britain and America, and in 1926 the first match was played at Wentworth, between a select British team and American players who were in England for the British Open at Lytham St. Ann's. Led by Walter Hagan in that first Ryder Cup match, the Americans were thoroughly trounced, but the idea was born and a schedule set up for the matches to be played the next year and after that, every other year, with the host country alternating between the two nations. Samuel Ryder set up a trust fund that would make available a solid gold cup of beautiful design for the biennial winners.

The first U.S. match was at Worcester Country Club in Massachusetts, and with the exception of the World War II years, the matches have been held since in the odd years. U.S. golfers chosen for the honor of playing on a Ryder Cup team (There is no monetary reward) are selected on a point system of wins and places on the PGA tour, with 70 points going for a win, 42 points for second place, and so on, down to 6 points for tenth place. The British have a similar pattern for selecting their players.

The matches had always been a two day affair, with 4 foursome matches of 36 holes one day and 8 singles matches the second day, each at 36 holes. At East Lake, for the first time, Ryder Cup became a 3-day tournament. The program stated: "This is the second major change in the Ryder Cup Matches in three years. In 1961, at St. Annes-On-Sea, England, all the matches were changed from 36 holes to 18 holes and the number of matches doubled.

"That streamlined format will be seen in the U.S. for the first time in 1963. It, and the addition of 4-ball matches, will add to the interest of contestants and spectators alike.

"Four 18-hole foursomes matches will be played on Friday morning, October 11 and four more that afternoon.

"In each foursomes match, two members of the American team and two members of the British team will oppose one another, each two man unit playing alternate shots with one ball.

"Four 18-hole matches will be played on Saturday morning, October 12, and 4 more that afternoon . . . each man playing his own ball and the better ball of each two man unit counting against the better ball of the opposing unit.

"Eight 18-hole singles matches will be played on Sunday morning, October 13, and 8 more that afternoon. In each singles match, one American and one British will meet under regular match play conditions."

Preceding the international matches, host pro Harold Sargent put on a Ryder Cup Program over his improved course. They

called it the Ryder Cup Pro-Am—actually it was played in April, six months before the big event. Most of the top players were in Augusta at that time of year for the Masters and most of them came back by East Lake for the Pro-Am, which was largely a fun affair for the pros as well as the amateurs, since the prize money was hardly more than enough to pay expenses.

The Pro-Am was won by the team of Julius Boros, playing with Charlie Harrison and John Shea, both AAC members, and William Branch. The winning foursome score was 59.

Total points in the Ryder Cup Match were shown as: Friday—U.S.—6, British 2. Saturday, U.S. 6, British 2; and Sunday U.S. 11, British 5, adding up to a final score of 23 to 9.

Crowds to see the tournament were estimated by officials and newsmen to vary between 7,500 and 12,000 for the various matches.

After the tournament Bobby Jones, who was on hand for most of it, wrote this letter to H.C. "Hikie" Allen, Jr.:

"I just thought I would tell you that there is not one single thing coming to my attention or notice about the Ryder Cup Matches that failed to give me pleasure. More specifically, the golf course was beautiful, the crowds well behaved and knowledgeable, the players skillful and attractive, and the general functioning as smooth as possible. This could not have been done without a lot of work and splendid organization.

"I am writing this identical letter to you and to Harold Sargent, since you were the two principally responsible for bringing the matches here and for having them done up in a style reflecting considerable credit upon the club and the town. Many thanks to you both."

The solid gold Ryder Cup trophy was retained by the Americans for the twelfth time in fifteen tries.

VI

Behind the Scenes

No history such as this would be complete without a record of those key people behind the scenes who dedicated themselves to a smooth and pleasant operation. Though I was not familiar with East Lake during the first 30 years of its existence, I have known it intimately for the last 50 years or more. From my own observation and from the very inadequate early records, the character and attractiveness of the country club and its members is very well expressed in the average length of service of its employees. Some served most of their working lifetimes there.

While there is not enough space to tell about all of these employees, those we can find in the early records, and those we remember, were typical in their devotion to East Lake.

In those formative years, East Lake seems to have had no club manager, as such. Apparently it was run by members assigned to committees and from the main AAC office downtown.

We can find no East Lake Club manager before George Bell. Bell had been with the Athletic Club for several years and was recognized as the President's right hand man. The East Lake clubhouse was drawing its largest crowds for golf, meals, dances and other social functions. Scott Hudson transferred Bell to East Lake in 1927. In the 14 years he served as manager of the country club, he helped to maintain it through the doldrums of the depression in the early 1930s.

When George Bell resigned, East Lake was without a resident manager for about two years. A.S. Hapholdt, who replaced Bell when he went from downtown AAC to East Lake, took over the management of both clubs. Hapholdt was a man with high qualifications for the job. He had graduated from Georgia Tech with a degree in commerce and business management, and when Mr.

Hudson found him, he was connected with the Biltmore Hotel. He had helped President Hudson bring the Athletic Club through the depression years of the '30s and was highly regarded in his profession.

The next manager at East lake was J.O. (Jimmy) Fischer. Jimmy came to the country club in May, 1942, with long hotel and public relations experiences behind him. He had served with the American Hotel Corporation for three years, then four years with Hotel Astor and International Casino in New York, where he was in charge of banquets and control of beverages. Later he was with Carl G. Fischer Corporation at Miami as manager of La Gorce Golf Club.

Jimmy and his attractive wife Mildred brought new activity to the East Lake club. They put on lavish Sunday and holiday buffets, Saturday night dinner dances with renowned orchestras, holiday parties, barbecues and other events that attracted a large segment of the membership and for almost two decades, gave East Lake one of its most popular periods. Often the enclosed terrace dining room and adjoining open deck were filled on week days when there was no special occasion. East Lake was conceded to be the most appealing of any country club in the metropolitan area.

Early in the 1960s, Jimmy Fischer resigned from the East Lake manager's position and was followed by a number of men, but in those days none of them were able to bring the grand old country club back to its days of its prosperity and glory.

There were those with lesser responsibility, but who stood as giants in helping the club run smoothly and efficiently over many years. Their contributions were possibly every bit as important, for they also dedicated a large portion of their lives to East Lake and its members.

One of our long time faithfuls was James Robert Brett. No club has ever had a better caddy master. Jimmy came to East Lake in the days before golf carts made a different game of golf. In the mid 1940s the game consisted of striking the ball and walking—not riding—between shots. Before the Brett era, there was always confusion around the golf shop door, with each swinger trying to get his favorite caddy, and the caddies making attempts to team up with a golfer who gave the largest tip. Brett soon straightened this out, and for 28 years at East Lake, and later at Riverbend, to which he was transferred when the club moved its seat of operations, he was one of the indispensible stalwarts.

If you were privileged to participate in the amazing game of golf back in the days before golf carts turned the game into a mech-

James Brett

anized affair, you know that one of the most valuable assets any golf club could have, was a qualified and efficient caddy master.

The jobs of always having enough caddies on hand, of keeping them satisfied and competent, of assigning them on an impartial basis, made up one of the most complex chores of this or any club. Jimmy Brett made it look so easy. If there was any friction at all, it was kept behind the scenes, so that the operation ran smoothly. We were generally unaware that it could, by any stretch of the imagination, be a problem.

When you were golfward bound and walked through the door into the golf shop, you met Jimmy Brett, gave him the names in your foursome, or told him how many players you needed to make your game. You ate lunch, changed clothes and completed whatever other activities were prelude to your play. In the meantime, if you needed players to complete your foursome, the caddy master who knew just about every one of the three or four hundred regular players, their handicaps and temperaments, and who they liked or did not like to play with, was sorting out golfers to find suitable players to fill out your game. If a qualified prospect came along, Jimmy handled the contact between him and the potential foursome in such a manner that almost without exception, any player or group of players could accept or turn down a game without embarrassment of any kind. And that, fellow hackers, was the essence of diplomacy!

Dave Williams kept the locker room at East Lake for almost half a century. Here is what was written about him shortly before his retirement when East Lake activities were transferred to Riverbend:

"No golf club is ever complete without a Dave. David Gartrell Williams—is the handsome, personable, scholarly-looking fellow who runs the locker room at East Lake Country Club. He is as much a part of the establishment as the lockers themselves, as the showers and the sturdy walls. To the 500 or more golfers who play a reasonable number of rounds over the two courses each year, Dave represents the 19th hole—the relaxation around the table when the woods and irons and putter have been tucked away in their bags for another day. He's the nursemaid, bartender, shoeshiner, matchmaker, attentive listener, gambler (but never more than a Coke or two on some hot big-league baseball game he has tuned in on his back room radio), and friend—and sometimes his job takes a lot of doing. Having Dave around gives you the same kind of comfort as taking off your heavy golf shoes after an especially trying round. When you need him, he's always there; to refresh

Dave Williams

61

you with that tall, frosted glass of lemonade; to pick up your golf shoes and replace them with a pair of street slippers; shined mirror-bright; to listen to your woeful tale of how you blew the last hole to lose a match."

David Gartrell Williams spent almost two-thirds of his entire life serving the members at East Lake. Back in 1924, before he reached his twentieth birthday, he came with the club when it was located on Auburn Avenue. Two years later when George Bell was

made manager of East Lake, he brought Dave along and placed him in command of the men's locker room, then located upstairs over the main dining room.

For more than a third of a century, in which he held the crying towel for the average East Lake duffer, Dave was friends with many of the golfing greats of America. Hagan, Hogan, Nelson, Snead and others passed his way at one time or another—and of course, our own Bob Jones, greatest of them all. Dave sweated out those championship years with Bob, and remained a staunch friend and admirer after the Grand Slam, when the maestro toured the East Lake courses for exercise and relaxation.

Among his friends the locker room chief could count many giants of industry and finance. He knew Senators and Governors and Kings—as King Leopold of Belgium, who dropped by once to play the No. 1 course he'd heard so much about. None of the caddies knew how to address him, so they simply called him "Mr. King."

"There wasn't nothing uppity about him," Dave confided. "He was just a fine gentlemen, the kind we like to have around."

Dave retired from East Lake when AAC sold this property and moved its golf to the new club at Riverbend. John Amos Hogue who had been assistant locker room attendant under Dave, took over and with A.P. (Red) Thomas served for a number of years until both retired.

VII

The Parting of the Ways
EAST LAKE SECEDES FROM
THE ATLANTA ATHLETIC CLUB

No one seems to know exactly when it started. The guesstimate by a number of individuals is that in the early 1950s, some of the Atlanta Athletic clubbers who lived on the north side of the city, began to talk about an additional golf course that would be more accessible and convenient to what they claimed was a majority of the members. The sentiment spread and when it developed to the point of suggesting that East Lake Country Club itself be surplanted by a northside installation, the lid blew off. Members who lived in Decatur and the northeast section of Atlanta made up almost as large a percentage of the membership as the northsiders, and the club arrayed itself as two factions that took opposite sides of the issue. One argument was that the rich tradition built up around East Lake over almost two-thirds of a century, would be violated, leaving AAC just another normal run-of-the-mill athletic club.

One of the influences behind the conception of Lanier Yacht Club was as a peace move to bring the two factions together by giving the northsiders a facility and keeping East Lake intact. To make East Lake more attractive in an attempt to keep everybody happy, improvements were made in the swimming arrangements, with a new bath house; much of the clubhouse building was remodeled and expanded; the tennis courts renovated; and the two golf courses put into as fine a shape as those of any club in the city.

For a while it worked. With sumptuous Sunday buffets, entertainment for all holidays, moonlight dances, extra service, the country club reached its peak of patronage. The dining room for both lunch and dinner was usually filled, and the men's grill was a busy place. Foursomes came to play golf while their families swam or played tennis, and then they all stayed to dinner. East Lake was a busy place and carried its share of the AAC financial load.

No one knows exactly when or why the country club began to deteriorate. Play on the golf course remained heavy, but the dinner and party crowds grew thin. Both food and service were still excellent, but the foursomes and others who used the club during the day, went home or somewhere else to dine.

Some blamed it on certain ethnological conditions; others claimed that AAC allowed East Lake to run down, to gain more support for a northside installation. Whatever it was, East Lake, as a total club, was on the way downhill, and that was when the north-of-Atlanta club again came into focus.

In the early 1960s, President H.C. Allen quietly appointed a committee to seek out available property in north Fulton County. The committee spent months examining tracts on both sides of the Chattahoochee River, as well as other sites large enough to fill the requirements of an overall country club. The recommendation finally boiled down to two large wooded areas. One of these had been looked over the decade before, and the 600 acres there turned down. It lay along the Norcross-Cumming road just west of the Chattahoochee River. The price per acre had gone up considerably in ten years, but this time, with soaring property values, it was considered a good buy. Acting in what it determined the best interests of the club, the Board of Directors took an option on what they hoped would be the site of the new country club installation.

The news of the newly optioned property did not cause as much commotion as had been anticipated. The general assumption was that the tract would be held for further expansion in the future. East Lake was intact, and this was the concern of those members living closest to it.

Events have a way of moving, sometimes slowly but always inexorably. The metropolitan area was growing, expanding, literally bursting at the seams. What wooded and vacant areas were left in the vicinity of the old club, mushroomed with middle to low class housing and shopping centers. The influx of humans brought added problems to the club. A certain element of the community resorted to nocturnal vandalism. Each dawn, when making their rounds, the greenskeepers found numbers of flagsticks bent around trees, cups torn out of the greens or worse, where some hoodlum had defecated into the cups. In a number of instances the greens themselves were torn by tire marks where vandals had skidded a car across the putting surface.

A part of this problem was solved by erecting a high woven fence around the clubhouse course. Number 2 course remained vulnerable. The cost of such a fence to enclose that area was not feasible, even in the face of such maintenance as was necessary to keep the second course in repair. The time had come to move and the Board moved quietly. The northside property, now known as Riverbend because it lay on a long arc of the Chattahoochee River, was purchased and a study or development committee comprised of Jim Shumate, Watts Gunn and Allen Harden (Shumate was later replaced by Oliver Saggus) was put to work on it. After the proper study was made, these men were to be assigned the responsibility of "handling the contract for the golf course, selecting and recommending to the Board an architect to work on the clubhouse plans and of handling this contract."

In March, 1966, the Board of Directors reported that the stockholders had authorized the sale of the No. 2 golf course "in order to provide funds for the construction of an additional facility on our Riverbend property."

The sale of the No. 2 course was not without its headaches. The stipulation of the potential buyers was that it had to be rezoned for housing development before they would purchase it. When this became known, a number of club members who were against the sale of the No. 2 course made an attempt to influence the County Zoning Board not to change the zoning status of the property. They threatened litigation. It was only through the efforts of some high-ranking and influential AAC members that the rezoning was accomplished and the property sold to Alex Smith and his group from Atlanta. The sale was completed to this group of local investors for a price which netted $1,000,000 to the club.

The schedule was that the new course at Riverbend and at least a working portion of the clubhouse, should be ready for play by the next spring. In the meanwhile, to keep from over-crowding the No. 1 course at East Lake, No. 2 was leased from its purchasers from March 1 through September 15, the months of heaviest play.

From the time the Riverbend property was purchased, the general conception was that the Atlanta Athletic Club would own and operate two golfing facilities, one for the convenience of its north and northwest members and the other to accommodate those living nearest to it in northeast Atlanta, Decatur and points east. The thought behind such a setup was that each course would get its share of play and neither would ever be too crowded. The Board and Club Managers worked hard to achieve this goal. Even after Riverbend was started, the old No. 1 course at East Lake was put into the finest condition of its existence, and in an attempt to reattract the luncheon and dinner crowds, much of the interior of the attractive English Tudor style club house was redecorated. In addition, the men's grill was converted into a trophy room, with members donating their prized specimens of their prowess, as

beautifully mounted marlin, sailfish, tarpon and a number of unusual game animals for the walls. Best chefs and waiters available were obtained and high quality food prepared. Special services were inaugurated, as bus service between the club and baseball and football games. The club went all out to keep East Lake a going concern, but in spite of all efforts, use of the facility, except for the golf play, fell off, and the club continued deeper into the red.

The decision was finally made by AAC's Board of Directors to sell East Lake properties. There was so much opposition to this sale that the directors called a special stockholders meeting on April 2, 1968 for a final and conclusive vote either for or against the sale of East Lake. The ballot count ran 900 in favor and 551 opposed.

"The northsiders outnumbered us," one Decatur golfer moaned.

East Lake was not disposed of without following through to a bitter end. Even after the special stockholders meeting, court action was taken by a minority of the membership to prevent AAC from selling its first country club property. This went its course through the legal channels before the courts granted final approval for the sale.

One concession that AAC made was that one or more Athletic Club members would be given the first opportunity to purchase the East Lake property. A number of those members held a meeting and talked it over. The unthinkable possibility was that some developer would desecrate the property with an apartment complex, destroying traditions and values built up over almost two thirds of a century.

The story of how East Lake was saved from the ignoble fate of being buried under crowded apartment complexes is a dramatic one.

A foursome of old East Lake members were sitting around the 19th hole in the locker room, bereaving the loss of the club and golf courses, and the fact that this could never be replaced. The more they discussed it, the more indignant they became, and that indignation grew into determination to do something about it.

Paul Grigsby was the spark plug. "Let's stop complaining," he said, "and get with it. We have enough AAC members who fought the sale of this East Lake property, who should be willing to get in on a partnership deal, buy this place and have a club of our own."

Grigsby was a highly successful business man. He had been a member and played East Lake since 1938. He was acquainted with most of the golfers and knew how dissatisfied they were with the way East Lake had been cast off by AAC with scarcely a shrug of the shoulders.

The foursome around his table that afternoon, and several other golfers relaxed nearby agreed that Grigsby's idea was sound and agreed to go along as partners in the venture. The Athletic Club has set a price tag of two million dollars on the property. Enough of those who enjoyed East Lake were financially able to help raise this much money and many of these said they would participate.

Grigsby went to AAC which gave him 90 days to raise the purchase price. East Lake's future seemed assured, but the picture was not as rosy as it had promised. Paul learned again what he already knew, that often those who talk the loudest come through with the least. Some of those who said they would help buy East Lake, decided to transfer their loyalties to the new AAC installation at Riverbend. Though Paul and a few close to him were fiercely persistent, they approached the deadline with only 25 investors who had pledged half a million dollars, only a fourth of the required purchase price.

Paul tried to make a loan for the balance, but none of the banks would touch it. Under all conditions of the time, the East Lake property did not appear to be a good investment, but Grigsby is not the kind of person who gives up easily. One man with sound business judgement and faith in the men who had dedicated their very existence to keeping an old tradition alive and active was W.O. Duvall, Chairman of Atlanta Federal Savings. He made a loan to Grigsby and his group of one million dollars.

This wasn't enough, but Paul took it. He went back to the directors of AAC and renegotiated his contract. The purchase price, which had stood at two million, was reduced to $1.8 million and AAC took a second mortgage for the remaining $300,000. Paul and his 24 partners and limited partners owned East Lake Country Club.

The road ahead of them was smooth at first. The Athletic Club which had not completed its golfing layout at Riverbend, leased the golf course at East Lake for the remainder of the 1968 season, and the rental was enough to keep the club rolling and the course in excellent playing shape. Then AAC opened one of its courses for play, the lease was cut off and East Lake was on its own.

The early 1970s were the rockiest years East Lake Country Club ever experienced. The new membership rolls, which had been estimated at 300, enough to keep the club well maintained, dropped to 50. Only a handful of golfers played the course. Use of the dining facilities was light. There was employees to be paid, maintenance, taxes, and substantial payments of interest and principle on the loan.

Paul Grigsby sold his business, retired and devoted his full time to East Lake. He solicited new members, he looked for new limited partners—anyone who might help him and his partners carry the burden. When payments became due, he and those partners who stood by him had to dig into their own pockets. It was a question of pure survival.

From the very beginning of the newly reorganized East Lake Country Club, Grigsby's No. 1 assistant and confidant was Marion L. Peek. Marion was a retiree from Reynolds Aluminum Company, and he stepped into the new club organization with many years of business experience behind him. From 1968 for the next several years, East Lake had no manager, but Marion Peek filled that gap as a supervisor of all facilities, including the clubhouse and maintenance and operation of the golf course. He handled the business statements from dues notices to accounts payable. He knew more about every phase of the club than any other person, and much of the success of East Lake is due to his diligence and long hours of work at the club.

Some of the original partners dropped out and charged off East Lake as a bad investment. Others stuck in there with Grigsby, providing enough money to barely keep the club alive. The cooks, waitresses, locker room attendants and course personnel who had elected to stay with East Lake rather than move on to Riverbend with AAC, came through with colors flying. Most had been with the country club for years and were dedicated to it. As individuals, they offered their services without pay, if the pinch came to that.

Among these long time employees was Jack Rollins, who came to East Lake as a cook in 1947. He was largely responsible for the success of many banquets, dinners and parties, and most individual members praised him highly for the excellence of the individual meals he prepared. When East Lake soared into prominence as a country club on its own, Jack remained as chef de cuisine. One of his specialities was the Friday night buffet which expanded as the membership grew and was a choice spot in the week's activities.

Another employee who had served the club since the middle 1930s was Mac Tomlinson. Mac was a purveyor of refreshments, liquid and otherwise. He had more contact with the golfers than Jack and his kitchen staff. For years one of his jobs was dispenser of bottle drinks and sandwiches at halfway house on No. 2 course on weekends, holidays, and on other days when play was heavier than normal. Every golfing member of the club knew Mac, and he knew most of them.

When No. 2 course was sold, the club built a halfway house near the putting green on No. 1 course, and Mac took over there. When play was too slow to keep a halfway house open, Mac was a special member of the clubhouse staff.

Mac retired in the early 1970s, but the years were lean for the club, and he came back to help out as a part time assistant in the kitchen and dining room.

"East Lake," he said, "has been my whole life. I never had any other job."

Morris Durrett came with East Lake in 1947 on a temporary basis; he took over full time five years later and was supervisor of food and beverages. He was another of those who could have transferred, but chose to stay with the old club. One of Paul Grigsby's right hands, he arranges and supervises all parties and special meetings.

Both Fanny Lyons and Barbara Martin had been popular waitresses at the club since the early 1960s. When the parent club moved on, they elected to remain at East Lake, although they were offered better jobs elsewhere.

John Amos Hogue, who had been an understudy of Dave Williams for many seasons, was given the opportunity to transfer to Riverbend, but turned it down to take the locker room responsibility under its new management. He kept A.P. (Red) Thomas with him until they both retired in the late 1970s.

Theo Jackson started working on the golf course in 1932 when he was 16 years old. This was the only job he never had and he wasn't about to give it up for another location. He stayed on with the new East Lake as grounds keeper and course maintenance man.

All of these people knew that East Lake—and their jobs—were on shaky ground. Even the boss, Paul Grigsby, could not guarantee how long the club might survive. But East Lake was a part of their lives, and their determination to keep the country club alive was as strong as Grigsby's. Their reward for helping it survive stemmed from love of the place and in giving of themselves, whatever the personal sacrifice.

Grigsby's obligation was not only his own long love affair with East Lake and to his partners who had joined him in the venture, but also to those faithful employees who had pledged to see the club through at any and all costs. This was a dark period and with it a frightening challenge of survival. The only solution to pull the club out of its red ink was as large a membership as possible. All partners worked at this assiduously, and the roster expanded, but some of these new members proved undesirable. They ran up large accounts both at golf and dining, paid no bills and had to be suspended and then cut off for non-payment of bills. The list of solid citizens continued to grow slowly but not fast enough to bring the club into the black figures.

For five years Paul Grigsby and his remaining partners continued to plug away, soliciting more members, selling an occasional new limited partnership, trying to fit a limited income into an overcrowded budget. Harvey L. Robertson, a local advertising man, was elected president of the expanding new membership in 1974 and was followed the next year by David Heinsma.

With these men actively at the helm, the membership increased substantially in the two years. It took a giant step when W.G. (Bill) Kallenberg came into the picture. Bill had been an active member of East Lake since 1973 and had worked steadily to help increase the membership and to spend much of his spare time doing chores to improve the appearance and usefulness of the club. It is said that he spent his entire vacation one summer rebuilding the boat dock.

Bill Kallenberg was a west Tennessean who had lived in Atlanta as a representative of Fidelity Distributors Corporation until he was transferred to the Company's home office in Boston. As a deep-rooted southerner, he kept his home in Avondale, near East Lake and commuted weekly to his job in Boston, where he became President of his company and chairman of its board. Weekends he spent most of his time at East Lake.

Though he did not actively retire from Fidelity Distributors until 1980, Kallenberg took on the presidency of East Lake in 1976 and 1977, and though he had only weekends at home, he threw himself whole-heartedly into building up the club and its membership.

Kallenberg was followed as President by Charles Allard and L.H. (Casey) Jones in 1978 and 1979. When he retired from Fidelity Distributors in 1980, he came back to East Lake as Chairman of the Executive Committee. With Harvey Robertson again as President, they set up a program that included promotion of special golfing activities and social affairs that increased the use of the club by its membership. New blood began to flow to East Lake. Initiation fees and dues were negligible compared to the other country clubs around the city. In addition, East Lake had an informality and friendliness about it that appealed to those who played golf or dined there, and the roster of members grew. When Kallenberg and Robertson turned over the reins of East Lake to Toby Sexton in 1984, the membership had more than doubled in the four years and stood at 500. The club was on its feet again and on its way back to the glory and prestige of earlier years.

The Kallenberg-Robertson team went several steps in helping Paul Grigsby put the club back on its feet. They organized teams to polish and dress up those areas most used by the members.

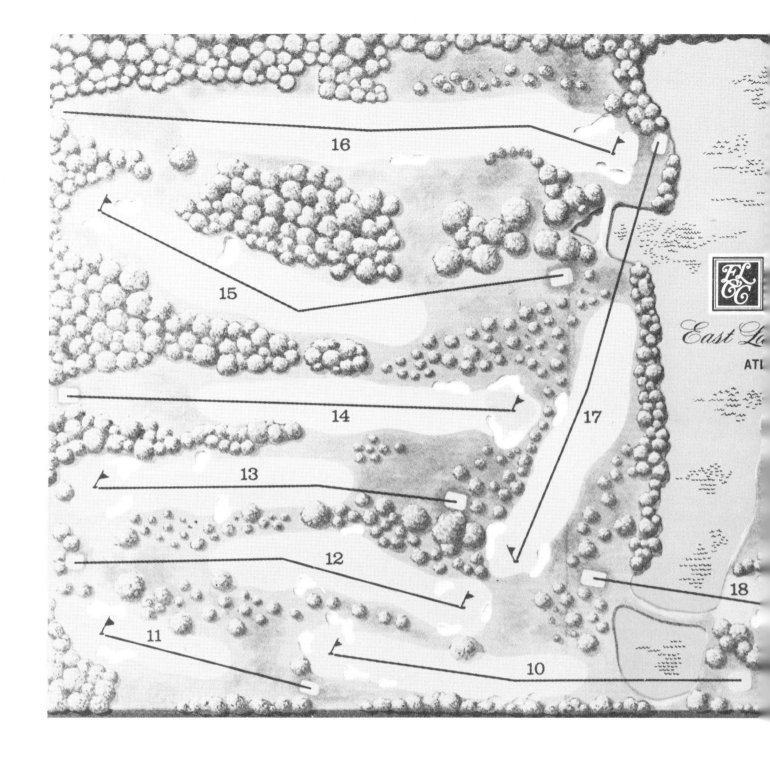

EAST LAKE'S

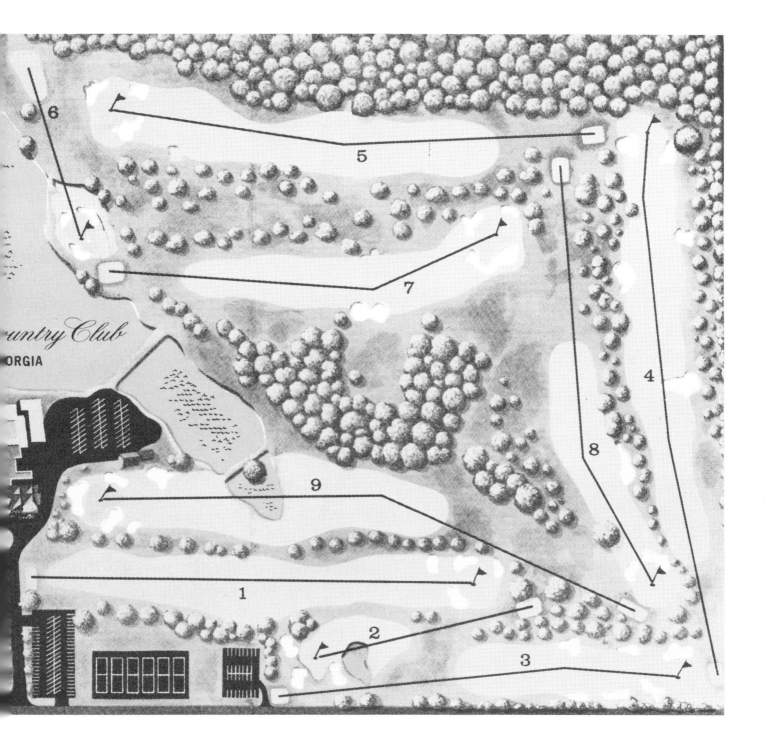

PRESENT GOLF COURSE

Much of the material for this was donated by other members. They added high class personnel to attend the members. One was Eddie Tukes, who was lured away from Druid Hills Country Club in 1978 and made head bartender at East Lake. It was a popular choice. The team also made provisions for part-time waiters and waitresses on those occasions when the clubhouse was in heavy use.

Golf pros had come and gone, among them Paul Bondeson and Dick Spain. In 1979 the Kallenberg-Robertson team came up with John Kirk who had been a very popular assistant pro at Druid Hills for seven years. By 1979 East Lake was beginning to show its muscles again, and John Kirk saw a good future there.

For five years he made invaluable contributions to building up the golf membership through tournaments and other competetion, and to supervising the course maintenance. His work with the course and with the membership attracted the attention of more prominent golfing organizations, and after five years at East Lake, he was offered a job with salary and potential that East Lake could in no way match. John Kirk was on his way to the big leagues of golf.

You stand now and look out over the broad sweep of the East Lake golf course. This, in golfdom, is hallowed ground. You are glad of two things: that it is not buried under the brick and mortar of condominiums, and that you are privileged to be a member of one of the world's most famous country clubs.

Index